FROM THE BRINK OF
DEATH
& THE GATES OF
HELL

JOSEPH HENTOSZ

authorHOUSE®

AuthorHouse™ UK
1663 Liberty Drive
Bloomington, IN 47403 USA
www.authorhouse.co.uk
Phone: UK TFN: 0800 0148641 (Toll Free inside the UK)
*   UK Local: 02036 956322 (+44 20 3695 6322 from outside the UK)*

Published by AuthorHouse   09/22/2020

ISBN: 978-1-6655-8046-5 (sc)
ISBN: 978-1-6655-8045-8 (hc)
ISBN: 978-1-6655-8047-2 (e)

INTRODUCTION

It is because off my maternal grandfather a highly decorated world war one hero who contacted a local North-West Lancashire (MP) who at that time in 1950 was a local (MP) for the northern seaside coastal resort county fylde town of North-West Lancashire the UK, were I was born and bred on the 20th July 1943 and also my eldest brother who was born on the 16th June 1942 in the UK, It was through his strenuous efforts that helped myself my English mother and her three young including myself English born children Escape from this vast enormous and extremely large country of Poland a country in East-Central Europe, it because of this MP and my maternal grandfather a world war one hero who sadly passed away and died in hospital from his war wounds in the year of 1968 that I am alive to be able to write my Memoirs "Meaning Memory" real-life actual Fact-based events true Story in this Book, Which is based on a true Story Title From The Brink Of Death And The Gates Of Hell,

To proceed with my fact based true events written story below it begins in the year of 1940,

[[THE YEAR WAS 1940]]

My story begins in the year of 1940 when my English mother first met noun meet this polish service man based somewhere in the busy north seaside resorts fylde coast and county town located somewhere in the vast large and enormous country of North-west Lancashire the UK, were I was born and bred in on the 20th July 1943 and my elder brother 16 June 1942, the tragic events that inspired me to start writing this tragic real-life actual events Fact-based story begins in the year of 1940 during world war two when my mother first met "meaning meet" in this busy northern seaside coastal resort, and fylde county town of this vast enormous and extremely large country of North-west Lancashire the UK, during world war two this young and handsome looking polish airforce service man who was stationed somewhere in the country of Northwest Lancashire the Uk, with the many different allied European countries forces during world war two, who were based in a military base somewhere in the vast and large country of North-west Lancashire the UK, To continue my dear mother told me that he was a handsome looking young polish airforce service man and she fell in love with him and he also fell in love with her and they started up a relationship together the year

1

was 1940 and through out her relationship with this handsome polish service man my English mother got pregnant twice sometime in the year of 1941 "first of all with my eldest brother who was born on the 16th June 1942 and myself who was born on the 20th July 1943 but because of the war he could be called back with the rest of the different European countries allied forces back into action so they both decided that they should get married before he goes back into action during world war two little did my mother know at that time during world war two what kind of a terrible devilish cruel abusive alcoholic drunken man she was going to marry, my dear brave courages English mother explained to me that she introduced her young and hand some looking young polish service man to her mother and father to inform them that they want to get married as she was pregnant again and she would like them to come with her and her polish boy friend to the local parish church, my now dearest late deceased English mother told me that both her father and mother agreed to go to the parish church with her and her polish boy friend and that it would be the best thing for there daughter to do now that she was pregnant once again so with that my mother and her young polish boy friend went with my mothers parents to see the church padre noun the title of a priest or chaplain to ask him if he would give them both his blessing to get married as soon as possible because of the war the padre agreed to give them both his blessing for them to get married and with in two days on a Saturday morning towards the end of the year of 1939 my dearest late deceased English mother told me they were married at this parish church based somewhere in the country of North-west Lancashire the UK, my English mother told me that the wedding and the day went quite well and after the wedding my mother and her now polish husband and her mother and father plus a few wedding guest's went across the road from the parish church to a public house for a wedding day celebration drink after an hour at this public house my mother told me that they ordered a taxi to take them both to a local B&B bed and breakfast guest house based somewhere in the country of North-west Lancashire the UK, that her polish boy friend had booked before they got married, "a room at this B&B "bed and breakfast guest house" for two nights only as he had only got a weekend pass from his polish airforce service unit and that he had to be back with his polish military service unit first thing on Monday morning with his military kit that's all he could tell my mother as his polish unit and the rest of the many European countries allied forces based some were in the vast and extremely large country of Lancashire the UK were going back into action and most were traveling by passenger express steam locomotive's from this busy northern seaside coastal county town and country of North-west Lancashire the UK, busy railway station, and the busy North-west Lancashire central railway station, were they were going too was top secret, so that was the last time she would see and be with him for sometime my dearest late deceased English mother told me that he did some how manage to send a couple of letters to my mother telling her that he well and if he is still alive when world war two finally ends and if he is still alive he won't be coming to see her because his polish military service Unit he was serving in will be returning back home to his vast and large country of Poland a country in East-Central Europe for demobilization noun to be releases from active service and demobbed, my English mother told me that after about three months she did received a letter from him and in the Letter he told my mother that he will be sending her some money for her to buy sailing tickets from a travel agency based somewhere in the northern seacoast county town and country of North-west Lancashire the UK, so that my English mother and her young children would be able to sail on a large passenger Liner from this seaport located somewhere in this vast enormous and extremely large country of Lancashire the UK, across this vast enormously and extremely large atlantic ocean to this polish seaport located somewhere in the vast and large country of

Poland a country in East–Central Europe, were my English mother's polish husband my polish father will be waiting for her and his young children who were born in the UK, to take us all in a taxi to his village were he lives located somewhere in this vast enormous large country of Poland a country in East-central Europe, after world war two had ended and he was demobbed noun discharged released from active service from the polish military service unit he served in during world war two as he promised my English mother in his letter he sent her the money to buy sailing tickets when my English mother did received the money from her polish husband she went to a travel agency office based somewhere in the northern seacoast county town and country of North-west Lancashire the UK, with her mother and father and booked and bought travel sailing tickets for her self and her English born children the sailing tickets were for us all to sail on a large passenger Liner berthed and moored in this sea-port based somewhere in the vast enormously large area of the country of Lancashire the UK,

[[THE YEAR WAS 1947]]

so towards the end of the year of 1947 we had to travel in the early hours of the morning at 6 am so my English mother told me on a express passenger steam locomotive from this Northwest Lancashire the UK, railway train station to this sea-port based somewhere in the enormously large country of Lancashire the UK, once there we will all board this large passenger liner, after saying good bye to her mother and father my dear English mother with her young English born children got on board this large passenger Liner, once we were all on board this large passenger liner we all stood together so my English mother told me when I was old enough to understand on the large passenger liners promenade deck to wave good bye to our

4

mothers father and mother as this ship sailed from this seaports dock, across the vast enormously and extremely large atlantic ocean in rough seas to this foreign seaport located somewhere in the vast enormously and extremely large country of Poland a country in East-Central Europe, My English mother explained to me when I was old enough to understand, about this near fatal incident that nearly happened to me while I was sitting in this high chair in the ships large dinning room were my dearest mother was trying to feed me, when suddenly a large wave hit the right hand side of this large passenger liner sending me flying out of this high chair across the ships large dinning room, I don't remember sitting in this high chair as I was just only a young child age about 4 years old at that time, it was my dearest Late deceased English mother that told me about this near tragic event incident that nearly happened to me, "being" tossed out of this childs high chair that I was sitting in that was next too the table that my mother was sitting at in this passenger ships dinning room which was full of the ships passengers eating food as this ship was sailing across the Atlantic ocean on rough seas it was being pounded by large waves, when all of a sudden this wave hit the side of this ship sending me flying out of this childs hight chair so my mother told me and that I was so lucky not to be injured or even killed as it was the quick thinking and quick action of one of the ships gentleman passenger who caught me before I hit the ships dinning rooms floor or even a dinning room table it was his quick reaction that saved my life, this is what my dearest Late long deceased English mother told me when I was old enough to understand, So began my tragic tormented and evil future life, I don't remember to much about this foreign seaport because I was just a young child aged 4 years old, I do not even remember seeing my English mothers polish husband my polish father waiting for us all to arrive at this foreign seaport, I don't even remember to much about our taxi journey with my English mothers polish husband my polish father in this taxi taking us all to his home in his polish village, I don't even remember to much about myself my mother and brothers sea journey across the vast enormous Atlantic ocean on this large passenger liner after this near fatal event that nearly happened to me on this ship, my English mother explained to me when I was old enough to understand that it was this ships gentleman passenger's quick reactions that I was not seriously injured or even possible killed, the rest of the journey on this large passenger liner was not to bad so my mother told me but she did not realize at the time that we were all sailing to a life of miserable living Hell, while living for two long terrible miserable painful abusive years from 1948 to 1950 in this polish village located somewhere in this vast enormous and extremely large country of Poland a country in East-Central Europe, My dearest brave and courgeous English mother was waiting for her polish husband to return from his polish mothers home which was above this horrible cold damp drafty rat-infested cellar, she looked at him and asked him if we are going to live in his mother house his reply was no as his mother told him that there is not enough room in her house for us all to live in her house and that the only other option left was the cellar below her house were your English family can live until you can find another place to live somewhere in this polish village, My English mother could not believe what he was telling her she looked at him and said to him that herself and her three English born young children had traveled and sailed all day and over night all the way from her families country of the UK, to be together as a family here in your polish village with you so what are we doing in this damp cold cellar, what the hell is going on and were do we eat live and sleep as we are all hungry and very tired after our long journey from the UK, his reply was that this cellar is your new home for a short time were you will live and eat and sleep until he can sort things out and try and find a better place for us all to live in my village, my mother said to him you must be joking there is not enough room for myself let alone our English born young children to sleep eat and live in together also I noticed that there is no electricity and no lighting and no heating and only one small window its so dark and miserable in this cellar and its really terrible cold and no heating how the hell do you expect us to live in these terrible cold damp freezing cold conditions in this cold cellar how do we eat as there is no electricity and no cooking facilities and how do you expect myself and you and our English children to sleep as there is only this one old smelly rotten bed that the Germans left behind his reply to my mother was don't worry as far as cooking food and heating goes I will find away to sort this situation out but this was not to happen as my dearest and brave English mother told me when we were all safely back home in our country of the UK, and I was old enough to understand that her husband turned into drinking and becoming an alcoholic and that in his drunken rage and state made him very bitter and angry against my English mother and her English born children which I think he regretted having them born in the country of the UK, so much that he became very angry and evil and in his drunken state of mind took it out on his English wife and her English children forgetting that they were also his half born polish and half born English Children by birth, to continue we had to bear and suffer is brutality for nearly two terrible painful years from 1948 to 1950" he used to hit my dear English mother his English wife knocking her onto the cold cellar concrete floor to stop her from stopping him from whipping myself and my eldest brother with this Leather thong Cat 'O' Nine Tail soaked in sea-salt water, noun a Cat 'O' Nine Tails Whip adjective meaning having Nine knotted whip cords thongs to enable it to bite into the skin, To continue after hitting and knocking my dearest mother onto the cold damp freezing old washroom one room cellar floor he then turned is attention in his drunken state of mind to me and my eldest brother he stripped me and my brother and whipped and abused us both with this leather thong Cat 'O' Nine Tale soaked in sea salt water to make the leather more harsh so as to enable it to bite into the skin he beat and whipped myself and my dear eldest late sadly deceased brother so many times for nearly two long painful torturous years in his alcoholic drunken state of mind but as time passed by myself and my brother became more tolerant verb meaning to endure and resist the pain of being Whipped with this Leather thong Cat 'O' Nine Tail Whip even though I was only five years old and my brother was only six years old we swore and made a pact noun a promise that if we are both still alive when we grow up and he is still alive we shall hunt him down and kill him as he is an drunken evil animal who does not deserve to live noun a pact adjective meaning that it is an agreement that when two people make a pact and a promise together such as myself and my eldest brother that we will suffer and try to bear this terrible suffering and excruciating pain and that one day we will both take our revenge on our abusive cruel drunken alcoholic father but at this specific moment in time we were like a fly caught in a spiders web and that is what its going to be like for the next two terrible tortuous painful abusive tragic years, towards the end of the year of 1947 and the start and beginning of the year of 1948 until the 2nd of October 1950 To continue on with my actual real-life events Fact-based true story which is based on actual real-life events that really did happen to myself, my dear late deceased eldest brother and our dearest and brave courageous English mother, that I will be writing about in this book from my memoirs "meaning memory" and also with the help of my dearest late tragically departed English mother who died and passed away tragically with terminal cancer, while I was holding her hand in this hospice It was at that precise moment that I once again faced death well over 30 years ago, I have faced and been close to the Brink of Death so many times, And yet I am still alive to write about it in this Book, It was at that moment that I do remember thinking to myself that what ever happens to me in my future life here in my country of the UK, I will never ever give into being abused tortured and the struggles of life and what ever happens I will be strong and death will never defeat me I shall face and fight evil and fight the battles and the many hardships and burdens of life and will do what my brave late deceased English mother wanted me to do and that is to write a book with the help of her dairy about my (our) life of Hell living with my English family in this horrible terrible evil cold damp rat infested freezing cellar and my nightmare flash back hellish dreams that I sometimes still have about me walking alone along this dark evil pathway towards the flaming gates of hell with the Image of the devil himself looking down upon me trying to force and entice me to enter the gates of hell it seemed so very real to me so real that I could even feel the intense heat coming from the Gates of Hell its only through my dear mother who poured some really cold over my face that I awoke and came out of this terrible night mare dream about walking towards the gates of Hell, My dear late deceased mother who passed away and died so tragically well over twenty years ago, explained to me that at that time when I was having this bad dream in this cellar she thought that I was really dying and close to the Brink of Death and that when she poured this really cold water over my face and I came too that she was so very happy and had tears of joy streaming from her eyes as she really though she had lossed me for ever as I was really close to the Brink of Death and dying, listening to my dear mother telling me this I could not hold back my emotions and tears flowed from my eyes and every time I think of my dearest brave courageous Mother who passed away and died so tragically well over twenty years ago with terminal cancer in a hospice, I cannot hold back my emotions and my tears as I still cannot forget how my dear brave and courageous mother suffered and struggled so hard to keep us all alive no matter what dangers she had to face, such as being continually stopped by the police and questioned for as much as three hours on end asking the same question over and over again which is better Poland or England they asked her time and time again, my dear English mother knew that if she said England she and her young children would never be seen again, its only because of her young English Children that They allowed the children to leave with there English mother only because they were a burden to the country, its difficult for me to compose myself and with strain my emotions when I think back about my English families escape from this foreign country in East-Central Europe, and how we escaped from certain death many times over, it was a long journey but we finaly escaped the path of death and returned back home to our country of the UK safely, with that in mind I decided to write these words of mine in this Fact-based Events True Story which relates to the title of this book from The Brink Of Death and the Gates Of Hell, that I am writing in this Real-life Fact-based events true story in this book' these words I write below in this book are not a poem as they have a true meaning about the Gates of Hell, The words that I have written and wrote below are not a poem and are based on this books Title From the Brink of Death and the Gates of Hell, "Hell and Death" I have faced Death and the Gates of Hell in the Face and walked away from both, Through out my life span, my pains my fears and the many sleepless nights painful nightmare dreams that stalks and haunts me day and night, an evil cloud of darkness surrounds me as I walk alone along this dark evil pathway, In my painful dreams towards the flaming Gates of Hell and a certain death, "Death and Hell" felt so very real to me that its hard to say this but I felt some how at peace and was not afraid of meeting death even though at that time I was a very young child aged 5 years old, It was my dearest Late deceased English mother that told me later on life that she thought I was dying and that she thought that I was close to the brink of death, and that she brought me back to life from this unbelievable and unimaginable nightmare dream of Hell, If it had not been for my dear mother pouring cold water over my face that I quite possible could have died as this evil death was that close to taking my life away from me, It was my English mother's quick reaction that quite possible saved my life that day, This all happened to myself and my (our) dearest brave and courageous English mother and her poorly and ill young children while all being forced to live in this small damp cold drafty freezing rat-infested smelly one room old washroom small cellar which had no electricity, lighting, heating, and no cooking or proper toilet facilities only some old rotting furniture and a smelly bed that the Germans had left in this horrible cella, this terrible situation we had to bear and suffer and live with for two long painful miserable years in this tiny village located somewhere in this vast enormously and extremely large country of Poland a country in East-Central Europe, for two terrible long painful torturous years towards the end of the year 1947 and the start and beginning of the year 1948 to 2nd October 1950, Its only because of my dearest late deceased English mother's dairy who passed away and died so tragically well over thirty years ago who was so ill with terminal cancer in a hospice, Its only through reading what she wrote in her private dairy, and also my sad unhappy memoirs meaning memory, that I am able to write the full Real-life actual events Fact-based true written Story in this Book Titled From the Brink of Death and the Gates of Hell, about myself my dearest late tragically deceased English mother and her young English born Childrens past miserable and abusive terrible tragic life that I have written and wrote about in this book which is based on an actual incident Fact-based true events story as told and written in the book title From The Brink of Death and the Gates of Hell, To continue I am beginning to find it a little difficult to continue on writing this story in this book as the memory of what happen to myself and my English family while being forced to live in this awful cold damp drafty and rat-infested freezing one room old washroom cellar in this village somewhere in this vast enormously large country of country in East-Central Europe, for two terrible painful abusive Poland a years from 1948 to 1950, is beginning to tear me apart and I feel so emotional, its difficult for me to hold back my tears, It was only while I was reading a story in this magazine about a young girl who wrote about her tragic life that I was inspired to carry on and continue writing this Fact-based events true story in this book Title From the Brink of Death and the Gates of Hell, Her story really did inspired me too regardless of my pains and my emotions to carry on and continue writing this Fact-based events true story that I have written and wrote about in this book, in my late deceased English mothers private dairy she wrote about her self working in a polish factory which was over two mile's or more from this village, were she was forbidden to sing or speak in English and had to walk over 2 mile's to this factory through treacherous snow blizzard definition a severe snow storm and freezing severe weather conditions because there was no transport at all, my dearest brave mother finished working at this factory because she was being taunted and persecuted because of her being English, also because my mother could not live on the £12 equivalent our mother earned working at this factory as milk was 3s.6d a pint and an egg 5s So we lived on any rotten meat sometimes my poor brave courageous English mother used to go out late at night so the villages sleeping people did not see her scavenging in this villages waist bins for discarded food such as any kind of meat and left over vegetables of any kind if lucky enough to find any such as potatoes which she used to heat in an old pan filled with water from this septic tank over these old paraffin lamps she found in this cellar that the Germans must have used, once the rotten meat and vegetables were hot enough to eat which we had to eat to keep us alive with dry bread and a cup of tea made with filthy water from a septic tank / eating this rotten maggot filled food helped mostly to try and stop us getting malnutrition even though we had already the signs of malnutrition noun the lack of proper malnutrition caused by not having enough proper and healthy food to eat, the only fresh food my mother could buy if she had the money to buy it was when at 5 o'clock every morning my mother and myself had to go out and stand for several hours in the severe cold ice snow blizzard definition a severe snow storm and freezing weather to queue for milk and if lucky butter but most of the time's we had to eat stale moldy bread maggot infested meat that I thought was still alive as it was moving this stale bread and rotten meat even though the stale bread and the rotting maggot infested meat was awful not only to look at and eat we still had to try and eat it even though it made us all feel very sick our dear English mother told us that it was the only way to survive as we all already had the signs of suffering with malnutrition so we had to keep our strength up by eating this smelly horrible rotten food but luck and fate was on our side as our mother was told by a person from a search party the news that they had found her polish husband and my (our) polish father dead in a freezing snow covered forest located somewhere in this vast enormously and extremely large country of Poland a country in East-Central Europe, My (our) wonderful brave unwell and exhausted very courageous adjective not deterred by danger or pain brave English mother told me that now your father has died we maybe have a slim chance to leave this terrible village and hopefully escape from Poland and return back home to the UK but unfortunately this person who my dearest brave courageous late deceased English mother told me when were all safely back home in our country the UK that he looked like an official type of person that came to see our unwell English mother and told her that because her polish husband is dead that herself and her English children have no legal rights to stay and live in this village or even any were such as a town or city or village any were or place in this vast and enormously large country of Poland a country based somewhere in East-Central Europe, as she and her English born children does not have polish citizenship or even hold a polish passport only a United

Kingdom of Great Britain Passport "my dear courages brave English mother explained to me when I was about 8 years old that she tried to tell this person that a child no matter what country that they live in and come from "born" to a polish parent is automatically a polish citizen at birth whether the child is born in Poland or elsewhere in the world this is what my dear English mother told me about and what she had written in her dairy she told me that this person told her that it makes no difference to him were we where all born that herself and her young English children will have to move from this village ASAP if not then he will have no other option but to have her and her English children arrested until they decide what to do with us all my English mother tried to explain to this person that her children were sick and ill as they were suffering from malnutrition and also from this deadly bacterial disease TB Tuberculosis, she asked this person how and were can she take her children in their poorly condition too in this snow blizzard storm and freezing cold weather they need to be and her self taken by ambulance to an emergency hospital for treatment by a doctor he told our mother that the only hospital near to this village is about 4 miles away and to get to it you have to walk a long way and through a forest which will take you about two hours or longer to reach the this hospital as there are no ambulances available or even near enough to take you and your children especially in the snow my mother asked this person are there any taxis in this village that can take us there his answer was no you will have to walk there with your children and its not his problem and not his fault that you and your English children are ill but you either leave this village in the next 30 minutes or I will have no option but to have you and your English children arrest by the police and put you and your children in prison until the officials can decide what to do with you our mother told this person you won't have to arrest us and that she will leave the village with her children as soon as she can in about ten minutes once she had packed what little items and clothes we all had to wear and that the only means of getting us to this hospital in the freezing bitter cold weather and deep snow was an old large sledge at the rear of this cellar that we lived in for two terrible long painful years that our mother noticed several times when she was hanging the washing out on the washing line with what little clothes we all had to wear that she had washed by hand in the oval tin tub that we some times bathed in, the sledge which was not used for a long time you could tell by looking at the very poor state it was in our mother was not to worried or bothered about the condition it was in as long as she can use it to get us all to this hospital, once our English mother had gathered what little items and clothing she pulled this old unused heavy sledge through the now deep snow to the cellar we lived in and put what little items we had onto the sledge and picked us up one by one onto the sledge and covered us all with the blankets she took from the very cold damp rat infested cellar we all had lived in for two terrible painful tragic years all the time this person was watching our sick unwell English mother who was ill and suffering from malnutrition who was struggling and trying to get us all onto this old sledge which she did with out his help because she new that he did not care and was waiting and watching out for any excuse to arrest us all my dearest brave and courages English mother was not stupid as she knew what this person was thinking that we would all perish and freeze to death in the freezing snow storm weather conditions some were along the way in this forest leading to this hospital as my brave courages stubbern English mother struggled to pull this old heavy sledge for 4 miles through the exstream server polish weather conditions ice deap snow freezing fog and the terrible snow blizzard towards this polish forest were this hospital was located in a sever blizzard snow storm, my dear and brave coureous English mother started to pull this old sledge with us on it through this deap snow she struggled a bit at first trying to pull the sledge through this deap snow but she would not give in and started to pull this sledge through the deap snow were my dear brave and coureous ill mother found the strength from to pull this heavy sledge with her three ill young English born children on it was "unbeleable" through the deap snow and the severe freezing polish winter weather, even though she was ill and suffering from malnutrition and this deadly bacterial desease TB-Tuberculosis, my dearest English mother knew that if she failed to get herself and her young children in time to this Hospital based in this freezing cold snow covered polish forest that they would either freeze to death or die from this deadly bacterial disease TB Tuberculosis, but she did manage to get us all safely and in time to this hospital in this polish forest when my mother finally arrived at this hospital some nurses who understood English helped carry our mother and us into the hospital once in side our mother was taken away from us to be seen by an hospital doctor, as for myself and my brother because were English children they decided that we would be to much of a burden to put us both in a childrens ward in this Hospital so they decided instead to put myself and my brother into this cellar below this Hospital until they decide what to they can do with us all, as we approached this cellar door I started crying and got very angry about being put into a cellar again and some how I managed to run away from the nurses and climbed on top of this wall on this hospital's balcony I looked down from the wall even though I was only 5 years old at that time I could see that the ground was a long way down and quite along drop from this hospital's balcony wall that I was standing on so if I decided to jump of this wall I would either be seriously injured or kill myself, the hospital's nurses knew this and tried to approach me to get me of this wall I told them to stay away from me as I will jump of this wall and that if they try to put me and my brother down into this hospital's cellar below this hospital that I would jump of the wall and kill myself as we had suffered enough cruelty and abuse while living for two miserable terrible long painful abusive years in this damp freezing rat infested one room old washroom cellar in our cruel abusive drunken alcoholic fathers village located somewhere in East-central Europe, To continue from above one of the nurses understood and could speak a little English and told me that every thing will be ok and if I would climb down of the wall but I did not believe her at first and threatened to jump and kill myself if any one came near me, I asked this English speaking nurse to tell these people who were trying to force my brother into this hospital cellar too let my brother go and stand by me and only then will I climb of this hospital corridor wall, she said something to the other nurses and looked at me and spoke to me in English for me to be very calm and that she is going to talk to someone to try and resolve this really dangerous serious situation, the other nurses and a doctor just stood there and looked at me and my brother after a short while the nurse came back with several other people she told me and my brother not to be scared that everything is going to be ok and that we are not going to be put into a cellar and that me my two brothers and our English mother are going to be given medicine by one of the doctors to help sustain and possible try to cure this contagious bacterial disease TB Tuberculosis in the mean time we are going to be moved into a hospital ward until we are all feeling a lot better then we shall be relocating from this hospital to a hotel were you will stay in until my English mother can get information about us all flying home to our glories country the UK sorted out but I noticed that my English mother's illness and health was not looking to good even though I was ill and not feeling very well I helped my mother look after my eldest brother who was really ill and close to dying while our mother had to go out of the hotel to try and get money by selling what little clothes we had left except what we had on to rise money to enable us all to return to our country of the UK, she was desperate for us all to escape and get out of this country somewhere in East-Central Europe, and return safely back home to our glories country the UK, My dear brave and courageous English mother was continually stopped by the police and questioned for as much as three hours on end they asked my (our) English mother time and time again the same question which is better Poland or England, my (our) dear brave and courageous English mother knew that if she had said England she knew that if she had said England that she would have been arrested and never seen again and her English children would have been arrested and possible never be seen again alive its only because they allowed her English children to leave only because they were a burden to the country that they decided to let my (our) English mother and her English children leave the country together which in away was good news but my (our) dear brave English mother was looking so very tired and ill and worried and did not know what else she could do even though we were all allowed to leave this foreign country and return back home to our country of the UK, as she had no money to pay for any plane tickets, She so worried because we were all seriously ill suffering from malnutrition and also with this deadly bacterial disease TB Tuberculosis that we would all possible end up dying together, in this foreign country but that would never happen as I shall never ever forget my dearest brave courages late deceased English mother who had to tolerate verb putting up with the many hours of being questioned by the police and the long delays which made my dearest brave courageous English mother feel really tired and ill, but she was a persistent and stubborn English women and would not give in and fight on to try and get herself and her ill young children out of this country in Europe and back home to safety to our country the UK, luckily one day my English mother came back with good news that we were able to fly back home to our country the UK and safety in an aircraft back home to our glories country the UK and hopefully safety I do remember this aircraft which flew myself and my English mother and her very young unwell looking English children back home to our country the UK, which had wooden seating on either side of the planes fuse large its mission was to fly myself my English mother and her English born family safely back home to our country the UK, I looked at my English mother sitting on this wooden seat on the right hand side of the planes rear fuselage, I could see that she was looking really tired and ill which I could understand after all we had been through and suffered for two long painful abusive miserable and torturous adjective involving pain and much suffering, for two long painful years from 1948 to 1950, And we were all still suffering from malnutrition and this deadly disease TB Tuberculosis,

[[THE YEAR WAS 1950 DATE 2ND OCTOBER]]

The date and month the 2nd of October the Year 1950 and our English families safe return back home to our country of the UK, after a long flight from this foreign country to our county of the UK we finally arrived and landed safely at this airport based somewhere in the UK, on the 2nd October 1950, when the aircraft reached the airports passengers terminal before we disembarked from the aircraft my English mother could not thank the air crafts pilot and the rest of the very kind and caring aircraft crew and told them that we shall never ever forget them all for the kindness and understanding and how they looked after us all with that over we departed from the aircraft and walked into the airports arrivals lounge were my mother told me that a Taxi driver was waiting for us that my mothers father my maternal grandfather had booked for her and her young English children to pick us up and drive us all to this busy northern seaside resorts coastal and fylde county town of north-west Lancashire the UK, I don't remember to much about the journey in this taxi as I fell asleep after about an hour or so we finally reached and approached the vast enormous large country of north-west Lancashire the UK, and as the taxi driver approached this busy northern seaside resorts fylde coastal town of Lancashire the UK, the taxi driver told my dear mother that her father had told him to bring us all to this amusement park were he worked when the taxi arrived at this amusement park my mothers father mother and Uncle were waiting for us to arrive when the taxi stopped my dearest brave courageous English mother got out of the taxi crying and shouting that she could not believe that herself and her English children are here and safe in the UK she was so tired and crying her mother and father got hold of there daughter to comfort her and asked her were are the children she said in the taxi on opening the taxi back door they found us scared crying and frightened lying on the taxi floor, upon seeing us they could not believe what they saw when they picked us up and held us in there arms how frightened petrified thin and fragile we looked they tried to speak to us in English but we did not understand them her daughter our English mother told them that at the moment we only understand and speak the polish language her mother replied get the taxi driver to take her self and her young children to her house were you will all live with us until you can get a council house to live in here in this town of North-west Lancashire the UK, so we went to live with my English mothers, mother and father in there home, it took myself and my elder brother quite sometime to get used to being treated well and eating proper cooked food, our dear grandma cooked us all a real Sunday lunch it was roast beef I asked my mother because I could not speak English properly yet what is roast beef and were does it grow and were are the maggots my grandma and grandfather both asked her daughter surely you did not eat rotten meat riddled with maggots my English mother my mother said yes as it was the only food we had to eat as I had no money to buy any food and no were in this small one room polish cellar to cook food, as myself and my three very young poorly English children could have died not only from malnutrition we had to eat this rotten food even though food looked terrible and was riddled with maggots it kept us all alive, the rotten food and eating the maggots helped to stop us dying of malnutrition, my poor young English children were to young to understand what maggots really were and thought they were meat I told them that they may taste funny but at first but we have to eat them to stop us all getting very poorly, ill and sick my two eldest English sons had a slight idea what maggots were they were both very brave and strong and started to eat the rotten maggot infested meat even though the were only a young children age 5 and 6 years old they both understood that they had to be strong and the only way that could happen was to eat the maggot filled rotten meat, any way back to my story my English mother explain to me what beef is and were it comes from so my mother explained to me in polish that beef does not grow like a flower I said what is a flower first she told me that beef comes from a cow and a flower you grow in the garden which you did not see in this village, my mother told us that as you grow up you will learn about nature and farm animals and how to grow flowers, my grandma and grandfather could not believe that we have never seen cows or flowers my mother told them as far as birds and animals and what farms there was you never saw any cows lambs sheep horses or birds or even any wild life any were near this village even Christmas was forgotten in this foreign village that we all lived in for two long years, Even her own young children did not known and understand what the tradition of celebrating Christmas was all about, My (our) mothers father my (our) maternal grandfather told us that in another two and a half months on the 24th of December it will be Christmas Eve and the next day 25th of December it will be Christmas Day but before then I will tell you a Christmas story then you will understand what Christmas is all about, My (our) maternal grandfather was a wonderful man a highly decorated world war one hero he could not understand and believe how we all could have survived for two years in this vast enormously large country of Poland a country in East-Central Europe, my mothers father looked at my mother and said these words we won the Last two world war's and our country of the united kingdoms freedom and yet you my dear and brave English daughter and your children suffered so much for two years while living in this foreign country its hard to believe that such things can still happen, my (our) mothers mother asked him to sit down and eat his Sunday lunch as there will be plenty of time to talk later on with that my dear mother told us to eat our Sunday lunch that our grandma had cooked for us all it was very tasty at first we enjoyed it but after a few mouth fulls it started to make me feel sick as my stomach was not used to eating and digesting freshly cooked meat and vegetables, As my stomach for two years was only used to eating rotting cold meat crawling with maggots and stale bread and horrible tea made with tepid sewer water boiled in a rusty old large tin over this oil burning lantern that was the only light and a little warmth we had in the damp very cold and freezing rat infested damp cellar, my (our) mothers father and her mother and uncle Billy could not believe it, until my (our) mother explained to them that her children's stomach was not used to eating and digesting real fresh meat cooked in a cooker, my (our) deceased maternal grandfather who was a world war One hero and a highly decorated soldier could not believe what my English mother his daughter was telling him, his words were if I remember rightly what the Hell I cannot believe what I am hearing do you mean to say that we basically won two world wars so that this country of the UK and its people could enjoy and still have freedom and yet from what you are telling me that you and your young English born children went to live in this foreign country somewhere in East-Central Europe for two years and like a slave you my daughter and your young children my grandchildren had to bear and suffering cruelty abuse and torture and basically starvation, and from what his daughter told him possible taken away and will never be seen alive again, my mothers father was so angry but also so very glad and happy that himself and this local MP who was at that time in the year of 1950 an MP for the country of North-East Lancashire the UK, managed to help them escape and get his daughter and her three young children out of this foreign country based somewhere in East-Central Europe, back home to there country of the UK safely, my maternal grandfather and our grandma and also uncle Billy my grandfathers brother really made all our lives wonderful and so very happy they could not do enough for us all as they both tought myself and my brother quite a lot, such as speaking English, and lots more, to help and get us ready to go to a primary school, which was only a few minutes walk from my grandma and grandads house and were my mother first met meaning (meet) our future step father who lived just around the corner from my mothers father and mothers home, When my (our) mother first introduced us to him he looked at us and the asked our dear mother what is wrong with them as they look frightened my dear mother explained to him about what had happened to them in Poland at the cruel and abusive hands of their deceased drunken and alcoholic polish father her polish husband who was thankfully found dead in a polish forest, he told her that he is so sorry that her children had suffered so much, I remember him looking at us with a few tears in his eyes and he knew that he had to give a little time for us to get used to him and trust him, which eventually myself and my dear brother did learn to trust him as he was such a kind and caring type of man who could not do enough for my mother and her children, and after a short while my mother and our soon to be step-father were married at this local parish church which was not far from her parents home in the country of north-west Lancashire the UK, which myself and my elder brother did not go to the wedding instead we were taken to a small church hall were myself and my elder brother were in the Boys Brigade learning about the promotion of habits, of obedience, reverence and discipline and self respect, and also to learn to speak our main language English, properly, and also to teach us myself and my elder brother god bless his heart to regain our confidence back in life and self respect and that not every person in this world is bad and evil, it was while we were attending the boys brigade parade our mother and our new stepfather came to collect me and my brother from the boys brigade parade to take us to our new home a council house located somewhere in this busy northern seaside resorts fyldes coastal town of north-west Lancashire the UK, the boys brigade officer in charge said to my mother that your children have settled and learned alot about being a true Christian also they have met noun meet and made a lot of new friends in the boys brigade once you have settled in your new home your sons will always be welcomed to attend the boys brigade again if the want to they are very nice and polite boys they both learn things very quickly and there English is getting better, myself and my brother went with our mother and her husband, our step father, so begins our new life together as things got a lot better at this point because our family was a lot more respected and our new step-father was an excellent step-father, and this semi detached three bedroom council house was situated in a wonderful area, and the neighbours that lived in this area were fantastic and caring as there was no animosity or strong hostility or racial slurs from the neighbours who really felt sorry for us and could not do enough for us as they had seen the photo of our mother myself and my two brothers in the local Evening Gazette news paper dated 2nd October 1950 and read the story about our escape back home to our country of the UK, I enjoyed living in our three bedroom council house so very much as from my bedroom window I could see lots of small and large famous Express passenger steam Locomotives which I had not seen before It was my dear Step-father who explained to me what a steam train was and that it pulls passenger coaches to take people to different places and that is how I learned all about steam trains, I was fascinated adjective of great interest magical enchanting charming and captivating watching and seeing the many different famous passenger express steam locomotives passing from my bedroom window, I really was catching up on lossed time and my education as I had so many thoughts and ideas of what I want to do in my future grown up life, One thing was for sure that I even sometimes forgot my tragic terrible painful abusive life in this foreign country a country somewhere in East-Central Europe, To continue with my story about this three bedroomed council house that we all lived in which was not to far from this busy seaside resorts coastal fylde town of north-west Lancashire the UK,

[[THE YEAR WAS 1952]]

After my family had settled into our new three bedroom council house myself and my dear brother went to this Infant Junior School located somewhere in the country of north-west Lancashire the UK, to learn and study English, unfortunately at this junior school we were bullied very badly with racial slurs against our polish roots myself and my eldest brother thought we were safe living in our country of the UK, but it was not to be so as our terrible and tragic ordeal we suffered while living for two painful terrible years in this foreign country based somewhere in East-Central Europe, was once again cursing and striking back at us we were in a very terrible state of mind and very frightened and crying for our mother to take us home so our mother with our stepfather went to see the local education authorities to see if they could relocate myself and my brother to another school our dearest mother and stepfather explained to the education authorities about the racial slurs and being bullied very badly at this infant Junior School it seamed to myself and my eldest brother that this evil death wish course had followed us all back to our country of the UK, our mother and step father only came to notice that some thing was terrible wrong with me as they found me hiding under the bed at night time crying and very very scared and frightened so much that they had trouble trying to get me from under the bed as I kept saying in polish Nie Nie Nie translated into English means no no no please don't beat and hit me with that whip I was frightened and having a terrible nightmare of walking towards the flaming Gates of Hell all over again because of the very unpleasant experience I had suffered as a young child aged 5 years while living and close to dying from malnutricain and this deadly bacterial virus disease TB Tuberculosis in this small one room washroom cold damp and freezing drafty rat-infested cellar in this polish village located somewhere in East-central Europe,

[[THE YEAR WAS 1953]]

To continue my English mother and step father was visited by the education authorities at this infant junior school to see what the problem was they were told that I was being bulled by some of the school children so the education authorities decided relocate me to another Junior school, and relocate my brother to another junior school situated just up the road from our home in which was much better and a lot more friendly and more helpful, after a little while I was also relocated to the same junior school to be with my brother as the head master of this junior school thought it would be much better and much happier for me to be together with my elder - brother at this other junior School as I was very frightened to mix and play with the School's young children after what happened to me at the first junior School at this point, we both felt comfortable, and happy and safe being together at the same junior school, I studied very hard and learned to speak English very well, also I was very good at learning quickly on many subjects but I am also not a theory type of person I am a practical person, while I was at this junior school I joined the ATC air training corps cadets I enjoyed it very much while I was in the ATC I learned quite alot about the RAF and its many trades, and also about the basic military training method, such as rifle drill close order marching military Style, my learning and education was improving all the time I have learned such a lot since I returning back home to the UK especially in the ATC aircadet training corps, were I learned to fly an aircraft at this airport somewhere in this North-west seaside coastal resorts Fylde county town and country of North-west Lancashire the UK, while serving as a cadet in the ATC aircadet training corps at this junior School in north-west Lancashire the UK, So I decided that when I was 16 years old I wanted to join and enlist into the R.A.F. and a new career, until then I was in the Life Boys Brigade for awail, then this junior school's ATC "aircadets" training corps finally after leaving the ATC aircadet training corp's I decided to join the Sea Cadet' Corp's to further my education about Navy Life, And finally I decided to join as a volunteer the TA territorial army 288 light ack ack anti aircraft guns to further my education about the three different armed forces services military life, especially the R.A.F. which I wish and want to enlist and join and serve in when I am 16 years old, I had come a long way since myself my mother and my eldest brother escaped from this vast enormously and extremely large country of Poland a country located somewhere in East-Central Europe, over 70 years ago and returned back to safety to our country of the UK, with the help of my hero my grandad a highly decorated world war One veteran and the help of an MP who at that time in the year of 1950 an (MP) for the county and country of Lancashire the UK it was only through both there strenous efforts that my once dearest late deceased brave and courages English mother and her three born young English children escaped from this terrible damp freezing rat infested freezing cold damp drafty small old wash room cellar in this village located somewhere in this vast enormous and extremely large country of Poland a country in East-central Europe,

[[DEATH APPEARS ONCE AGAIN IN MY LIFE]]

The following actual real-life events Fact-based true story that I have written and wrote is based on my most magical treasured childhood Memoirs "Meaning Memory" is about the 50s 60s and the 70s, when as a young boy aged 8 years old, I watched and learned a lot from my now sadly and tragically deceased Step-father who was a wonderful kind and caring father who died so sadly and tragically from a broken heart when he lossed his wife my mother who passed away and died so tragically with terminal cancer, It seams to me that I shall be facing death in the face for the rest of my life and for some reason unknown to myself I keep on walking away from death, To continue my dear Step-father tought me quite a lot about what his job was as a TV and Wireless engineer such as repairing the old 1950s valve televisions sets and the old 1950s valve radios all this I learned while watching my step father repair the 1950s valve televisions and the old 1950s old valve radios my step father was a top engineer working as a television engineer for a TV and radio company situated in this north coast seaside resort and fylde coastal county town located somewhere in the vast and enormous large country of North-west Lancashire the UK,

[[THE YEAR WAS 1954]]

I learned quite a lot in such a short time by helping my late tragically late deceased step-father who I miss so very much as I do my brave mother as every time I look at there photographs tears fill my eyes but the memoirs meaning 'memory' of our happy times together brings a smile to me face, my dear step father who was a wonderful caring and kind man showed me how to repair many old 1950s televisions and radios which I learned to do very quickly, it was a very exciting time in my life as a young boy age 8 years old repairing the old 1950s tvs and radios that were not working my dear late deceased step father who died of a broken heart after the tragic death of his wife my dearest wonderful brave courages English mother who died so tragically with terminal cancer, my (our) step father was a real wonderful kind man who died of a broken heart not long after the tragic death of his wife, my mother, who as a young boy age 8 years old I used to help my mother with money by working as a paper boy at this local newsagents and confectionary shop based somewhere in the country of North-west Lancashire the UK, which was not far from the council house myself and my family lived in this was my first job in which I delivered the morning and the evening news papers from the news agents confectionary shop to the shops local customers homes in all kinds of weather in which I earned money at the age of 8 years old to help my now long dearest late tragically deceased English mother to buy food and towards paying the rent ext before I went to school, most of the money I used to earn delivering the morning and evening news papers to the papershops customers homes I gave to my mother to help her buy food and coal for the living room coal fire as my mother could not work at that time because she was pregnant at weekends and on school holidays after I finished with my early morning paper round, I also had another part time job working as a delivery boy for a butchers shop based somewhere in the country of north-west Lancashire the UK, delivering up to 30 plus meat orders to the many busy B&B bed and breakfast guest houses and the many busy sea front promenade hotel's on this butchers shops old 1940s delivery bike which had a large basket at the front of the butchers shop deliver bike, to place the specially wrapped moisture vapor proof heavily waxed freezer laminated paper wrapped meat orders into the very large butchers shops deliver bikes very large basket which could hold and carry up to 30 plus careful wrapped in moisture vapor proof heavily waxed freezer special laminated paper wrapped meat orders which made the basket and the butchers shops delivery bike very heavy to ride and control as it was a 1940s old butchers shop delivery bike as in the following story that I am writing as follows on below about this old butchers Shops, delivery bike which was an old butchers delivery bike dated around the 1940s it had a large wheel at the rear of the old butchers bike and a small wheel at the front of the butchers shops bike with the large wicker basket placed above the bikes front small wheel has shown in the following picture further on below it was very difficult to ride and control the small front wheel with the bikes handlebars because the weight of the many different packed meat orders in the really large wicker basket which was standing in the low gravity metal carrier above the bikes small front wheel made the front wheel of the bike difficult to control and stear properly and quite a few times I lossed control of the bike and fell of the bike which fell on top of me and a quite few of the carefully wrapped meat orders fell out of the delivery bikes large wicker basket onto the streets road side as I was trying to stear and turn the butchers delivery bike on to the street were I had to deliver three carefully wrapped meat orders to three bed and breakfast guest houses located on the same street who had ordered and paid for the meat joints I had to deliver to them which was now lying on the side of the streets road side luckily the driver of a car which was just passing me managed to avoid hitting and running over me and the bike the driver of the car stopped and got out of his car to see if I was ok and not injured I told him that I am ok and that I had only grazed my hand and my head slightly but when I tried to get up I could not as the heavy butchers bike which still had alot of wrapped meat orders I still had to deliver still in the really large wicker basket which was lying on top of me the driver of the car that nearly hit and run over me with the help of some holiday makers who were sitting out side of the B&B "bed and breakfast guest house" that they were staying in across the street from were I fell of the bike came across to see if I was ok and helped the driver of the car remove the heavy butchers bike of me and then helped me to get up and then helped me to pick the wrapped meat joints up and put them back into the butchers shop delivery bike's large basket again fortunately as luck would have it the weather was good and the meat orders were not damaged because of the special moisters vapor proof heavily waxed freezer's specially laminated paper wrapping once the driver of the car that nearly hit me knew that I was ok and not injured got into his car and drove off, the bed and breakfast guest house owners who came out side to see what was going on approached me also to see if I was ok I told them yes I am ok and that I must continue with my butchers meat deliveries they asked me what butchers do I work for I told them that I work for butchers shop located in the town they said that I must have there meat order in the basket so told them to look at the meat orders in the basket and sure enough there meat order was there so I handed it to them they thanked me and asked me if I would like a cup of tea and a little rest after my accident I replied no thank you very much as I have a lot of meat orders to delivery today I thanked them for there concern as I did with there holiday guests and continued with my meat orders deliveries thinking back to that day I was very lucky that I was not injured or killed but as I was lying on the pavement with the heavy old 1940s butchers delivery bike lying on top of me in that specific precise moment for a few seconds It felt like I was once again close to the Brink of Death, after a little while I continued on with delivering my meat orders to the rest of the many B&B bed & breakfast guest houses and the many busy hotels with no further complications or accidents I was very glad to finish all of my many days deliveries and return back to the local butchers shop that I worked for as a delivery boy, as I walked into the butchers shop the manager who had already heard about my accident was really concerned and worried about me and asked me if I was ok I replied I am fine just a couple of grazes but I am ok, the butchers shops manager asked me what happened I told him that the delivery bikes small wheel could not really handle the heavy weight of the many different wrapped meat orders in the large basket he understood and told me not to worry as he had already contacted the butches shop's head office for a new up to date butchers shop delivery bike with proper large front and rear wheels and a proper medium sized basket which is going be delivered later today before we close which was good news to me as the old butchers bike I used to ride with a really large wicker basket the 30 or more virius different meat joints were put in the really large wicker basket which sat in the low gravity carrier which was above the bikes small wheel at the front of the butchers shops deliver bike, when full of the 30 or more virius different meat orders because of the weight of the 30 plus different meat orders in the old 1940s butchers bikes large wicker basket which sits in the bikes metal square carrier above the old 1940s butchers bike front small wheel made the butchers bike quite heavy and difficult to ride and control and to steer the bike's front small wheel to the right of the very old vintage 1940s butchers shops delivery bike The new 1950s butchers shop deliver bike with a much better medium size wicker basket with specially strong 22 inch rear and front wheels which replaced the old vintage 1940s Butchers Shops delivery bike which I struggled to control because of the weight of the 30 or plus specially wrapped moisture vapor proof heavily waxed freezer specially laminated paper wraps meat orders from then butchers shop into the large basket to deliver to the country of north-west Lancashires the UK, seaside resort towns many bed and breakfast houses and the many busy hotels I really enjoyed riding the new 1950s butchers shops delivery bike as it was much better and a lot easer to ride and control because of the much specially strong 22 inch front wheel and the medium sized wicker basket helped me make my butchers shops meat orders deliveries much quicker and a lot safer I did learn quite a lot from the county and country of Lancashires UK butchers shop such as the fine art of butchery such as slicing bacon on the butchers shops large meat and bacon slicer also the fine art of making pork sausages from lean raw pork shoulder once I have removed all of the bones and then chopping into small pieces the raw pork shoulder and then putting it through the butchers shops large electric meat mincer and sausage maker also the fine heart of recognising the different cuts of beef pork cuts and the basic lamb cuts it was a delicate and very scillful art and could take months even years to learn the fine art of butchery I quickly learned most of it and enjoyed learning the scilful art of butchery which possible could come in very handy one day in the near future, I worked for this butchers shop as there delivery boy delivering the customers meat orders I worked at this butchers shop until I was 15 years old and I left school in the year of 1959

[[THE YEAR WAS 1959]]

And my first job I got after I left school at the young age of fifteen years old was working at this busy luxury hotel as a commis waiter to learn the special art of lying the Imperial Hotels many dinning room tables, My first day on my new Job as a commis waiter the dinning rooms senior head waiter told me to follow him across the dinning room to a section were there was three dinning room tables, he looked at me and said this will be your serving sector verb area were you will be serving the hotel special guests, he looked at me and told me don't worry I will be teaching you for the next week or so the fine art of Silver Service and how to prepare and lay the three tables with clean special white satin tablecloths and show you the correct and proper way to place the Silver Service cutlery on the three tables clean white satin tablecloths once we have done that we will get ready to serve the early morning hotels VIP guests breakfast, after the early morning breakfast had finished the head waiter then showed me how to replace my three tables with fresh clean satin table cloths and then reset the Silver Service cutlery the proper and correct way on the now fresh clean white satin tablecloths, After a weeks training the hotels senior head waiter who trained me for a week the fine art of silver service lying on my three dinning rooms tables stood and watched me to make quite sure that I had learned from him the proper way of lying the Silver Service correctly on my three dinning room tables and how quickly I could do it when I had finished lying and setting up my three dinning rooms tables and cleaned the hotels large dinning rooms carpet with a vacuum cleaner he told me that I was quick to learn the hotels large dinning rooms fine art of Silver and that I was very popular with the hotel guest's as I made them laugh, and that I should eventually get a promotion to become a fully fledged hotel silver service waiter, I really enjoyed my job at this hotel as a silver services waiter but after working at this large sea front Hotel for about fifteen months located somewhere in North-west Lancashire the UK, I decided to hand in my notice even though I met meaning meet many famous people who offered me a job position working for them such as one famous racehorse owner offered me job as one of his jockeys but for the first three months as a stable boy and training to ride horses to become a jockey which

I turned down as I did not want to be famous, because my main mission in life was when I was old enough to enlist and join the R.A.F. So until that day arrives I wanted to further my education in another job position,

[[THE YEAR WAS 1961]]

To continue from above applied for a job working at another sea front Hotel I was lucky as I managed to secure this position as a page boy at this Hotel, my duties as a page boy first of all was to clean this Hotels main entrance front door's brass name plate ever morning then I had to hover and clean the large carpet as you entered into the hotels foyer noun main reception area once I had finished hovering the hotels reception area my next and most important job as this hotels only page boy was to help carry the Hotels guest baggages onto the hotels manual controlled lift that I was trained to operate which would take them up to the floors were the hotels many rooms were located, it was a very interested job as I met meaning meet a lot of people and I also made a lot of friends especially the hotels head door man who trained and showed me how to operate the hotels manual controlled lift and what a page boys daily duties and responsibilities and the daily tasks were every day, he was a kind and wonderful person I got on quite well with him its such a long time ago that I have forgotten his name do remember that he lived not far from were I lived, he told me one day that he remembers reading one day this news paper headlines with his wife dated 2nd of October 1950 about myself and my mother's terrible miserable painful life and ordeal living in this foreign country in East-Central Europe, with my mother and her three young children, he told me that his wife felt really sorry for us all and if she can do anything for us please ask her, I thanked him and asked him to also thank his wife for her kindness, and that the story in the news paper was only a small version of what my mother told this local Lancashire news paper reporter and that one day sometime in the near future I will be writing a book with the true and full story in it, the hotels head door man said to me that when you do write the full and true story in a book and its being published he will buy a copy for him and his wife to read I told him that he does not have to buy a copy of the finished book as I will give him a free copy of the book he replied that he will look forward to reading the book he asked my what will the title of the book be I had to think for a minute or too and then suddenly a thought came to mind about the title of this book which was about my night mare flash back dreams about me as a young child walking towards the Gates of Hell and certain Death, So the title of this book shall be From the Brink of Death and the Gates of Hell, my good dear friend the head doorman of this hotel looked at me and said thats a Hell of a title myself and my good wife shall be looking forward to reading the book, Unfortunately a few days later after speaking to my good friend the hotels head front door man about the book I shall be writing when I grow up it shall be to late for him to read as a couple of days later when I arrived at the Hotel to do my duties as the hotels page boy I was informed that the head doorman my very good friend had died during the night time it was his very upset wife who had telephoned the Hotel that she as always tried to wake her husband up to get ready for work but no mater how hard she tried to wake him up there was no response so she called the emergency services for an emergency ambulance to come quickly to attend her husband who she could not wake up with in a matter of minutes an emergency ambulance arrived at her house with a doctor who upon checking her husband he told her that he had died sometime during the night I could not believe it he was such a very gentle and nice person it upset me so much that the hotels manager told me to go home and take the rest of day of which I did, I keep on asking myself the same question over and over why do I more or less loose every one that I have known pass away and die tragically, the only explanation that I can think of is an explanation which is a statement about how or why something is the way it is such as I am still cursed with this evil death wish curse that has stalked, hounded and pursued me relentlessly for over 71 years or longer, what baffles me the most is the fact that I was born on the 20th July 1943 and that I will be 77 years old on the 20th July this year 2020 and I am still alive even though I have faced death in the face many times over and over even though during in my specific younger years I suffered with specific medical conditions, noun various types of illnesses and injuries and I was really close to the brink of death on several occasions such as I sustained an injury during my active service in the R.A.F. and I also suffered with a serious sunstroke while I was on a three month detachment overseas in a R.A.F. Station located somewhere in the vast enormously and extremely large area of the Sahara desert of Libya, it was only through the quick thinking of an R.A.F. medical airman that I am alive today as he recognized the symptoms that I was suffering with such as being very hot flushed and having really dry skin he felt my forehead he found it very hot but I was not sweating I was more or less unconscious and drifting in and out of unconsciousness he realized straight away that I was suffering with heat stroke also known as sunstroke which is the most serious form of heat injury and is considered a medical emergency and that I needed urgent medical attention and treatment ASAP he immediately alerted the R.A.F. stations medical center hospital who immediately sent the R.A.F. Stations hospitals emergency ambulance to rush me to the medical centers hospital were this R.A.F. medical doctor told me that I was suffering with severe heat stroke also known as sunstroke which if not treated quickly can either kill you or cause damage to the brain and other internal organs, he explained to me that heat stroke results from prolonged exposure to high temperatures usually in combination with dehydration which leads to failure of the ebodys temperature control system a dangerous condition that results when your body temperature gets to hot greater than 104 degrees Fahrenheit and is considered a medical emergency it was only the quick thinking of this R.A.F. service airman who actually saved my life, whilest I was serving on a three month detachment at this R.A.F. station based somewhere in the vast enormous and extremely large area of the Arabian desert of Libya. I have so far been lucky and cheated death on several occasions but this evil damnation evil death wish curse, meaning to wish for something evil or unpleasant to happen to someone, such as the tragic and sudden death of my good friend this hotels head doorman who after his funeral I decided to hand in my months notice to the hotels general manager to leave my job as this hotels page boy he told me that he will be sorry to see me go as you are a really intelligent kind and caring young lad and will go a long way in any job I explained to him that I want to join the R.A.F. and to dedicate my life to serve my country of the UK, In any way that I can do even if it means fighting and dying for me country of the UK, I shook this Hotels general managers hand and left the Hotel,

[[THE YEAR WAS 1962]]

After I finished working at this hotel as a page boy, I finally decided to volunteer and join the R.A.F. which I did and had a new career job serving the Queen and her Royal Family and the people of this country of the UK, in the R.A.F. and so it came to pass that at the young age of 16 years old I finally received my rail travel warrant to report to this No: 7 school of new recruit's training R.AF. Station based somewhere near the farmlands of this vast enormously large area of the country and county of West-central Shropshire, a country in the UK, so during the early hours of the next morning I boarded a passenger express steam Locomotive located at this northern busy seaside resorts fylde coastal town train station of the country of North-west Lancashire the UK, to travel to another and my final destination train station located somewhere in the UK, traveling on the same train there was some other new R.A.F. Recruites who had enlisted and joined the R.A.F. who were traveling on the same passenger express steam locomotive that I was traveling and heading towards this railway station located somewhere in the vast enormously large country and county of Shropshire the UK, Once we arrived at this train station we had to report to this R.A.F. Station's Number 7 School of Recrute Training which was based somewhere in the vast enormously large country of Shropshire' As we all departed from the train there was an R.A.F. Corporal waiting for us on the train stations platform he said to us right lads form a line he had a clip board in his hand and called our our names one by one when he was satisfied that we were all here he said follow me and he took us all across the road from train station to a hotel were we had to wait for this R.A.F. military services transport coach to arrive to take us all to this R.A.F Stations Number 7 School of Recrute Training, to our surprise at the hotel there was refreshments waiting for us sandwiches and cups of tea after our very long long journey's from our different cities - country side villages and towns in the UK, while we waited for this R.A.F. stations military services transport coach to arrive after awail the R.A.F. Corporal told us that the R.A.F. Coach will be arriving shortly when the R.A.F. coach finally arrived he shouted right lads grab your suitcases and follow me out side and get on board this R.A.F. coach which is going to take us all to this R.A.F. Station Number 7 School OF Recrute Training, when we finally arrived at the R.A.F. Stations Number 7 School OF Recrute Training, my new career and new life in the R.A.F. was about too begin, after we settled down in the R.A.F. stations holding barracks hut, the

R.A.F. stations senior sergeant physical training instructor told us to fall in out side as he was going to march us all to the stations R.A.F. clothing department store when we arrived there the R.A.F. Sargeant Instructor in charge of the new R.A.F. recruites training told us this is were we fit you all out with your new R.A.F. uniforms and your bedding once you are all kitted out you will all fall in out side to march you back to the R.A.F. stations holding barracks hut for a short time and then you will all march with your R.A.F. service kit to your new quarters the R.A.F. stations barracks hut were you will live and sleep in for the next eight weeks then the R.A.F. Stations School of new recrutes training sargeant told us all that this is were your physical harsh eight weeks tough intense training begins and your lives are going to change for the better we were then all marched to the R.A.F. stations school of new recruit training Stations Squadron holding barracks hut for two days until we received our R.A.F. kit the next day after we were we drew our R.A.F. service kit, we were all marched to this R.A.F. stations new recrute's Hut 126 (Barracks) which will be our home for the next eight weeks of intense strict and tough training, I was really looking forward to getting started with the intense strict training and square bashing for the next eight weeks intense training in all kinds of weather sleat hail snow rain and freezing conditions, finally after myself and my friends had completed and finished the tough intense eight weeks training at this R.A.F. stations new recruite's training school, which we all passed with flying colours, our last and final mission was before we all depart from this R.A.F. station's number 7 school of new recruit training, was our passing out parade in which for the final and last time we all marched with the stations airforce band playing the R.A.F. march, with lots of pride, after our passing out parade in front of the many parents and families and the stations commanding officer who was attending the passing out Parade, and after the passing out parade finished we were all marched to the R.A.F. stations photography office to have our passport photographs taken once our photographs were taken and developed they were placed in all our R.A.F. UK, passports, after we were handed our new R.A.F. UK passports, from there we all attend our final pay parade to receive our R.A.F. pay and train travel warrant, also we were all allocated our R.A.F. postings to different R.A.F. Stations both in the UK, and also on active service to the different R.A.F Stations based Overseas, once I received my R.A.F. pay and train travel warrant I boarded the R.A.F. stations military services transport coach to take myself and my R.A.F. friends who were traveling by train back home to were they lived in the UK, and myself back home to my country of Lancashire the UK, were I was born and bred on the 20ᵗʰ July 1943 for a months leave before I fly to my new posting from this R.A.F. transport command Station based somewhere in this vast enormously and extremely large country side of Wiltshire, to fly from there on this R.A.F. transport command military aircraft to fly myself and other military service personal overseas on active service to this R.A.F. Station based somewhere in the vast enormous and extremely large area of the Arabian desert of Saudi-Arabia,

[[THE YEAR WAS 1962]]

To continue after I said good bye to my mother and my wonderful step father and my two step sisters and step brother I got into this taxi my mother had booked for me to take me to this train station to catch and board a passenger express steam locomotive which will take me to this railway station based somewhere in the county and country of Lancashire the UK and from there I should be able to catch and board a train to take me to a railway train station based somewhere in the country side and county of Wiltshire the UK after a long journey on this passenger express steam locomotive we finally arrived at this railway train station based somewhere in the country and county of Wiltshire the UK, after I got off the train at this train station I approached a station porter and asked him were the bus station was he told me just across the road from this station you cannot miss it with that I walked out of the train station and crossed the road to the bus station once there I asked a bus inspector what bus do I catch to take me to this R.A.F. station based somewhere in the country side of Wiltshire's picturesque charming country side farming village he said and pointed to a green Wiltshire bus I thanked him and made my way to the green Wiltshire bus were the condutor and bus driver was standing smoking a cigarette as was a beautiful warm sunny morning I asked the bus conductor if this is the right bus to take me to this R.A.F. Transport Command Station based somewhere in this large farming village based somewhere in the vast enormously and extremely large country side of Wiltshire the UK, he answer yes mate it is you are just in time as we are just about to leave with that I boarded the bus and went up stairs to look out of buses window to admire the charming scenic picturesque beautiful sunny morning Wiltshire country side view it was a wonderful and most magnificent magical site to behold, after awaile the conductor came up stairs and I paid him for a bus ticket and asked him if he would let me know when we arrive at this R.A.F. station he said ok pal no problem after about 20 or so minutes journey on this bus we finally approached this large Wiltshire farming village and this R.A.F. transport command station, the bus conductor came up stairs and said to me we are approaching the R.A.F. stations main gate enterance bus stop I thanked him and I got of the bus at the bus stop which was just across the road from the main enterance leading into this R.A.F. transport commands station as I walked through the main enterance on the left was the R.A.F. stations military provost guard house were I had to report to show my R.A.F. Identity Card and the documents with details of my posting overseas to serve on active service at this overseases R.A.F. station based somewhere in the vast enormous and extremely large area of the Arabian desert of Saudi Arabia, this R.A.F. transport command station's military provost (MP) looked at me and said to me well airman every thing is in order, but you will not be flying overseas to your new posting until the early hours of tomorrow morning about 6 am I asked him were will I be staying today he told to me that you will be staying like the other R.A.F. service airmen and the other military personal posted on active services overseas to this R.A.F. Station, also this R.A.F. military MP told me that until your flight in the early hours of the next morning at 6 am you will be staying over night at the stations inflight overnight accommodation which which is at the very top of the station you cannot miss it, after spending the night in the R.A.F. Stations inflight accommodation and after eating and finishing our early morning breakfast in the airmens mess myself and the other airmen made our way to the R.A.F. Stations airfield were we finally boarded the R.A.F. stations military transport aircraft at 5am in the morning once we were all on board the R.A.F. military aircraft it took off at 6am and our 11+ hour flights long journey to this overseas R.A.F. station, After about 11+ hours of flying we finnaly approached and flew over this vast enormous and extremely large are of the Arabian deserts of Saudi -Arabia, it was a magnificent site to see, we finally arrived and landed on this R.A.F. stations airport runway after an eleven hour's flight to my new posting on active service at this overseas R.A.F. Station based somewhere in the Arabian desert of Saudi Arabia, When we finally landed at this R.A.F. overseas Station and the passenger pressurized door was opened and we disembarked from this aircraft, the heat out side was un'beleavable the temperature in the afternoon in the Arabian desert of Saudi-Arabia can be severly hot with average high temperatures reaching 36 degrees celsius (96.8 degrees fahrenhert) and overnight temperatures are generally usually very hot with an average low of 28 degrees Celsius (82.4 fahrenhert, after myself and the rest of the military and the R.A.F. service men disembarked from the aircraft, We were all told to follow this R.A.F. corporal to the R.A.F. station's holding barracks were we shall stay for a couple of days until we were sorted and transfered to our new different R.A.F. units, for two days we just relaxed and tried to get used to R.A.F. desert heat of 36 degrees Celsius (96.8 degrees fahrenhert) and the night time temparture of 28 degrees Celsius (82.4 fahrenhert I found out that it rains less than once a year in Saudi-Arabia after two days we were finally relocated to our different R.A.F. units so began my two and a half years posting to this overseas R.A.F. station based somewhere in the vast enormous and extremely large area of the Arabian desert of Saudi-Arabia, I served for two and a half years at this R.A.F. overseas Station based somewhere in the vast enormously large area of the Arabian desert of Saudi-Arabia, I realy enjoyed it while I was serving in this R.A.F. overseas Station, that was until this overseas R.A.F. Station that I was stationed and serving at in Saudi-Arabia was put on a state of emergency, but even though this overseas RAF Station based somewhere in the Arabian desert of Saudi-Arabia was on a high security allert threat level indicating the likelihood of a possible terrorist attack at any moment, which I was trained for during the course of my 8 weeks training, I still enjoyed serving overseas on active service at this overseas R.A.F. Station based somewhere in the vast and enormously large area of the Arabian desert of Saudi-Arabia I made alot of good friends while I was stationed for two and a half years at this overseas R.A.F. Station, I remember well that the year was 1963 when myself and some of my R.A.F. friends decided to have a day out on our day off to this Saudi-Arabian city based opisit this Saudi-Arabian major cargo seaport city, and after having a good day out and a few drinks we made our way back to the R.A.F. Station but instead of taking an arab taxi we decided to walk back to the overseas R.A.F. Station as it was not to far and as always the night sky was clear and it was as always in Saudi-Arabia a very hot night and as we were walking along I suddenly fell down a six foot hole just missing by inches a large spike sticking out of the sand which grazed my side near my heart, a few inches more it could have possible gone through my heart once again I had faced death in the face and I was that close again to the Brink Of Death and quite possible the Gates of Hell, there was no sign's or even red lights warning people that road and pavement works were in progress, I was very lucky to be alive, my R.A.F. friends helped pull out of the deap hole and as I lay down on the sand they noticed that I was bleeding on the left side of my body on the side of my body were my heart his situated they feared the worse case scenario that my heart had been pierced by this spike and they were going to call for a R.A.F. emergency ambulance, I shouted to them no I am ok I thing its just grazed my skin with that they helped me to remove my shirt and sure enough luckly the sharp spike had only grazed my skin cutting it and causing it to bleed a little nothing to serious to be concerned or anxious about, with that we got a Arab taxi to take us all back to the R.A.F. Station were I at once went to the stations sick quarters, were a R.A.F. medic looked at were the spike had grazed the part of my upper body he looked at me and said that its only a slight cut I will give you an injection of penicillin but first of all I will need to phone the duty medical officer for his permission to give you this penicillin injection after awail the duty sick quarters medic returned and gave me the penicillin injection noun this medication is used to treat a wide variety of bacterial infections especially from rusty metal objects, after he gave me the penicillin injection he placed a large plaster across the small wound to help stop the bleeding I thanked him and made my way to the stations service mens club luckly I was ok and once again I had faced death in the face and walked away from it,

[[THE YEAR WAS 1965]]

Good things do finally come too and end as after serving for nearly two and half years on active service at this oversease R.A.F. Station based somewhere in the vast enormous and extremely large area of the Arabian desert of Saudi-Arabia on active service I received an order from the relocation posing officer to see him upon seeing him he told me that I am being posted back to the UK, on a months leave and during the course of my months leave I should receive an official letter with an authorized military railway warrant included and also including an official document letter regarding the travel details of my new posting to this UK, R.A.F. transport command station based in this country side large farming village located in somewhere this vast enormous land extremely large country of Wiltshire a country in the UK, It was while I was stationed and serving at this R.A.F. Transport Command Station that I met meaning meet my now late sadly and tragically deceased future beautiful wife who passed away and died so terrible and tragically on the 12th August 2001 at such a young age she was only 45 years of age when she died, who's funeral took place nine days later on the 20th August 2001, we were married on the 26th October 1968 and we were happily married for 35 years and new each other for 40 wonderful magic happy years my dearest late beautiful wife was to me a beautiful flower and blossomed and bloomed in my heart every day like a red rose we fell deeply in love with each other at first site which lasted for over 35 wonderful happy years my dearest late tragically deceased wife was introduced to me by an R.A.F. Officer's daughter who I was friends with and who was a friend of my late deceased wife told me that she would bring her girl friend to the station's service mens and service womens club so that we could get together and introduce our selves and see what myself and my R.A.F. officers daughter's girl friend think of each other well needless to say upon meeting each other in this station's service mens and service womens club it was love at first sight and we started courting each other,

[[THE YEAR WAS 1967]]

To continue from above I received orders that I am being posted from this R.A.F. Transport Command Station that I am serving at in the UK overseas on a months detachment on active service to an overseas R.A.F. Station based somewhere in this vast enormous and extremely large Sahara desert of Libya, I explained to my girl friend that I have received orders that am being sent overseas on a month detachment too this overseas R.A.F. Station, my girl friend looked worried I asked her what is wrong she told me that she was worried that I would forget her, I told her not to worry as I shall think about her all of the time and carry a photograph of her next to my heart while I am away on active service oversease on a month detachment, I told my girl friend that on my return in a months time to this R.A.F. Transport Command Station, I want you my future wife to be to arrange to meet me with your girl friend in the R.A.F. stations service mens and service womens club for a drink and to talk to her about our future life together' she said ok I will but she had a few tears in her eyes I told her not to worry we will be together for a long time once I return back from overseas from my months detachment, So with that over the next day myself and several other R.A.F. personal were transported on an R.A.F. personal service military transport bus to an unown decommissioned old war time once R.A.F. airfield some were in the UK upon arrival at the airfield the R.A.F. transport bus stopped near a waiting R.A.F. Aircraft which was ready to leave the airfield and fly us all to our destination to this overseas R.A.F. Station somewhere in the vast enormous and extremely large area of the Sahara desert of Libya, once we were all seated the R.A.F. aircrew flight sergeant welcomed us all aboard the R.A.F. Aircraft and then he called out our names one by one from a clip board he had in his hand, once he was sure that every official R.A.F. personal on his list was on board the aircraft he told the R.A.F. officer pilot in charge -the go ahead to take off from the airfield, at last and finally we took off from this decommissioned world war two R.A.F. airfield somewhere in the UK, and fly us all overseas to our destination this overseas R.A.F. station based somewhere in the vast enormous and extremely large area of the Sahara desert of Libya, via this overseas R.A.F. Station based somewhere on this remote and small maltese Island were we will land for a few hours or so to refuel our aircraft, after flying for about hours from the UK, we were finally approaching this overseas R.A.F. Station based somewhere on this remote and small maltese Island were we should land for a few hours to refuel the R.A.F. Aircraft, and also so we can stretch our legs and get something to eat, but an emergency happened as we were on the final glide path or glide slope approach noun which is the last leg in an aircrafts approach to landing when the aircraft is lined up with the runway and descending for landing at this R.A.F. Station's runway located on this remote and small maltese Island but as our aircraft approached this R.A.F. Station's airports runway it suddenly started to shake violently and was being pulled dangerously down by the hot air rising upwards from the intense heat rising upwards from the hot deserts sands which can act like a magnet and possible pull an aircraft sharply down on its final glide paths approach while trying to land on a airfield runway we all thought that our plane was going to crash and hit the ground hard and that we will all be killed I just could not believe that this was happening to me again I could not comprehend verb grasp mentally understand that I survived danger and faced death as a young child many times over I could not believe that once again I was facing death in the face but by a stroke of luck and a miracle our

R.A.F. pilot managed to at the very last moment with only a few feet to spare pulled our aircraft sharply upwards away from the deserts ground and made an emergency landing on this overseas R.A.F. Station's airfield runway and after the R.A.F. officer pilot had landed the aircraft safely and taxed his aircraft safely to a stop he came out of the aircrafts cockpit and asked us is every one ok we replied yes sir a little bit scared but ok thanks to your skill as an R.A.F. airforce pilot he explained to us what had happened that as the aircraft was approaching the airports runway it suddenly hit an hot air pocket rising upwards from the hot desert sands thats why our aircraft started to shake violently which as caused the aircrafts navigation system to malfunction and possible cause the aircraft to crash but we are trained well to expect and over come situations such as this one, but unfortunately it means that until the navigation system is replaced in this aircraft we cannot continue on with the flight today to your posting to this overseas R.A.F. Station, until tomorrow the R.A.F. Pilot told us so I suggest that you relax and get something to eat and if you have never visited before go out and visit the maltese town you will find its full of history and very romantic your over night accomodation as been arranged at this overseas R.A.F. Station so with that we all departed from this R.A.F. aircraft to get some thing to eat and after we had something to eat we all headed to this town in a taxi, after having a good time in the town and visiting a few good night clubs in the town we headed back to this R.A.F. Station in a taxi to enjoy a good nights sleep and an early morning breakfast and hopefully our flight from this overseas RAF Station, to do and complete our four weeks active service detachment at this overseas R.A.F. Station based somewhere in the vast enormous and extremely large area of this Sahara desert of Libya, as we were eating our early morning breakfast this R.A.F. Aircrafts Aircrew Flight Sargeant came into this R.A.F. Station inflights mess dining room to inform us all that this aircraft navigation system as been replaced and any other electrical problems have been sorted out and this aircraft is now ready and safe to take off and complete the flight journey to your posting overseas to this RAF Station, so gentlemen please follow me to board this aircraft as the pilot is waiting to take off to complete our flight to your destination this overseas R.A.F. Station to start and complete our four weeks detachment tour of duty at this overseas R.A.F. Station, when we finally arrived at this overseas R.A.F. Station and landed at the stations airfield and as we departed from this aircraft an R.A.F. transport bus was waiting to take us all to this R.A.F. stations temporary barrack huts when we arrived at the stations temporary barrack huts, this station's staff sargeant was waiting for us he showed us all into our temporary barrack huts and told us that we could relax for the rest of today and tomorrow you will report to your different units were you will carry on with your normal R.A.F. duties for the next three weeks, so with that over I suggested that in stead of us all going to the stations service mens club for a drink why not take a trip on this Arabian Bus waiting out side of the R.A.F. Stations main entrance gate to go to an Arabian town in stead and visit and have a drink in an Arabian bar they all said thats not a bad idea lets all go so with that we all got on a this Arabian bus that was waiting out side the stations main guard room gates were all had to show or R.A.F. Identity Cards before we could leave the station and board this Arabian bus to take us to an Arabian town or Arabian village when we finally arrived in this Arabian town we all got of the bus and walked through this very quite Arabian town we saw an open Arabian bar so we went into the Arabian bar and ordered a drink luckily the Arab bar man who was standing behind the bar understood the English language and poured us a drink of Tiger beer which was nearly 100% proof in alcohol as we stood at this Arab Bar I asked the Arab bar man how do we get to the beach and the red sea he replied as you go out of the door turn left and walk a few paces and turn left again and just keep walking straight on you will see the beach and the red sea in front of you I thanked him and followed his instructions as we neared the white sandy covered beach and saw the Red Sea which was a magnificent adjective impressive site to see any way we carried on walking until we were standing on the white coloured Arabian sandy beach little did we realize that we had walk over an old German disused mine field as there was no warning signs around this area we decided to cross it as we could not see any other way to get to the beach after we finally reached the white covered Arabian sandy beach and the Red Sea with no incident and soon we were walking on this white covered sandy beach and the red sea not far from this small Arabian town and the Arabian Bar but there was not much to see or do and the sun was very very hot so we decided to return on a Arabian Bus back to the R.A.F. Station were we were all stationed at on a four weeks detachment to take a shower to cool down and then after a shower go to the the R.A.F. Stations service mens club for a drink after I finished having a cold shower I walked back to the temporary R.A.F. Stations barracks hut to have a few moments rest on my bunk bed before meeting my friends in the R.A.F. stations service mens club for a drink but tragity was about to strike me once again as the next thing that I remember was waking up in a bed in the stations sick quarters were I was confused and feeling very dizzy my eyes were blurred and my vision was sort of misty all that I could see and feel some person or persons removing most of my clothing and gently applying cool water and fanning me and some one placing ice packs on my body to bring my temperature down to a safe and normal level, they also stuck a needle in my arm so that fluids and medicines will flow through my bloodstream through an intravenous drip, I just could not understand what was happening to me after a little while I was told by R.A.F. Stations sickquartes medical doctor that I had collapsed in my hut on my bunk bed suffering with very sever and serous sunstroke you are very lucky to be still alive as it was the quick action of a qualified R.A.F. medic who was on the same four weeks detachment posting the same as you and staying in the same barracks hut as you who recognised the serous sever symptoms of heatstroke that you was suffering with he at once contacted the stations sick quarters and told the stations sick quarters duty medic that this is an emergency call and that an RAF Service man who is here on a four weeks duty detachment posting from an R.A.F. Station in England is in a very serous condition suffering with sever sunstroke his symptoms are headache dizziness and weakness extremely high fever and the absence of sweating he also told the stations sick quarters duty medic that with out prompt and adequate medical treatment the sunstroke can be fatal and cause a sudden loss of consciousness and in extreme cases it may be fatal and cause death he told the sick quarters medic that he knows this as the symptoms are that upon feeling my forehead I was really very hot and burning up but not sweating, he thinks that my body temperature is at a dangerous level of between 108 F and may rise as high as 112"F (42 to 44.5 "C) or even higher also that he was confused and feeling agitated his speach was slurred and also that he was suffering with delirium seizures and he was in and out of a coma, also his breathing is very rapid and that with out prompt and adequate treatment the sunstroke can be fatal and cause instant death he needs immediate prompt urgent medical attention the duty R.A.F. Stations medic told him that I am on my way in the R.A.F. Stations R.A.F. Emergeny Ambulance and that he will be arriving at the hut soon I was a patient in the R.A.F. Station sick quarters for a couple of weeks during that time I suffered with delirium causing me to have flashbacks of myself standing at the Gates of Hell once again Noun a flashback is when memories of a past trauma feels as if they are taking place in the current moment and of a traumatic incidents that I experienced at a specific time and place, after two weeks as a patient in this overseas R.A.F. Stations sick quarters I fully recovered my temperature was back to normal I was discharged and returned back to my duties, it was a very close call as once again I had faced death in the face and walked away from it, Its was the quick reactions of this R.A.F. qualified medic that I am still alive he deserves a medal for his actions in saving my life, what I cannot understand and it baffles me is the fact that I served at this other over seases R.A.F. Station based somewhere in this vast enormous and extremely large Arabian desert of Saudi - Arabia for two and a half years were temperatures can reach as high as 36 degrees Celsius, 96.8 degrees Fahrenheit, and even higher, you could fry an egg on a swimming pool baths concrete wall, or even on a cars bonnet, it was so hot that if you tried to use a hosepipe to wash your car, before the water could reach the car it would have turned into steam, thats how hot is was, there is a big difference in the temperature at this R.A.F. Station based somewhere in the vast enormous and extremely large Sahara desert of Libya, were the temperature reading is a lot lower and is between 24+ degrees Celsius -19+ degrees Fahrenhert which is a lot cooler then it was when I was serving for two and a half years 1962 to 1950 at this other over seases R.A.F. Station based somewhere in the vast enormous and extremely large Arabian desert of Saudi-Arabia were the temperature reading was a lot higher and could reach as high as 36 degrees Celsius – 96.8 degrees Fahrenhert and even higher,

[[THE YEAR WAS 1967]]

To continue after a months detachment at this overseases R.A.F. Station on active service, were once again I faced death in the face and walked away from it I returned back home to the UK, and to my normal duties at this R.A.F. Transport Command Station based somewhere in this pictuesque scenic charming Wiltshire country side farming village located somewhere in the county and country side of Wiltshire a country in the UK, After a long flight our aircraft finally Landed at this Transport Command R.AF. Stations runway and after it finally came to a stop, I felt quite happy it was a good flight and I was looking forward to departing the aircraft and dropping off my R.A.F. kit bag into to my R.A.F. quarters, I then went straight to the stations service mens club for a drink at the bar with my R.A.F. friends I did not notice my friend this officers daughter sitting with my girl friend in the R.A.F. Stations Military Service Personel's Club because I was standing at the service personnel's clubs bar having a drink with my R.A.F. friends at the bar to my surprise my friend who was an R.A.F. officers daughter who introduced me to her girl friend approached me at the bar and said to me hello welcome back home are you ok I replied yes then she asked me why are you ignoring my girl friend who is upset and is sitting over there pointing at her girl friend who she introduced me to I explained to my friend that I have only just got of this R.A.F. stations aircraft that I flew here in from my months detachment overseas, and it was a tiring and a thirsty long flight and all I could think of was that I needed a drink of beer and a cigarette thats why I came straight to the bar and that's is the reason why I did not see you or your girl friend who you introduced me too when I walked in my sincere apologies to you both please go over and ask your girl friend to come over to the bar as I want to introduce her to my R.A.F. friends at the bar and also I need to talk to her about our future life together so my friend the R.A.F. officers daughter went over to her girl friend and brought her to the bar I looked at her and told that I am sorry that I have upset her and that I did not see her when I came into the R.A.F. stations'service mens club I looked at this R.A.F. officers daughter who was my friend and thanked her for bringing her girl friend over to me and I asked her and her girl friend if they would like a drink she said no thank you and that she had made other arrangements with some of her friends to go too the town located somewhere in the county and country side of Wiltshire for a night out I thanked her for looking after my hopeful new girl friend to be thats ok and I know now that my girl friend will be very happy being with you and she would love to be your girl friend and possible more than that for ever and with that she left to go and meet her other girl friends so after she left I introduced my new girl friend to my R.A.F. friends at the bar who told her that I am a lucky person as she his a beautiful looking young girl I looked at her and she was smiling at me and it was love at first sight and that was the start of our long term relationship together and we started courting each other for about a year or so we were so very happy together and so very much in love with each other that we got engaged and at the same time I asked her if she would like to marry me she said yes straight away so we started to plan our wedding day and our future life together as husband and wife, we both decided to get married on the 26th of October 1968 at the R.A.F. station's and the large country side farming villages Church, we were both very happy and looking forward to that very special wedding day, at first we both thought that it was going to be a wonderful magical and happy occasion and I thought that at long last my life is going to change and that I will not encounter verb unexpectedly be faced with or experience an hostile force such as death, but I was so very wrong as once again tradgity and death was about to strike me once again as I received the most tragic news about my eternal grandfather who was critically ill and dying in Hospital located somewhere in the county and vast enormous large country side area of Lancashire the UK from a telephone call that I received from my English mother on the 24th October 1968 two days before myself and my future wife's wedding day on the 26th October 1968 informing me that my Hero my maternal grandfather a world war one highly decorated hero was lying in Hospital in a critical condition and dying from his world war one battle field war wounds that he received as a world war one stretcher bearer whilest going into the battle field time and again to try and save as many of his wounded or badly injured comrades as he could even though he was wounded him self many times and bleeding my eternal grandfather did not like to talk much about what he did during in world war one as a soldier and a stretcher bearer, because of his heroism and valour noun great bravery and great courage in the face of danger especially in battle, He showed me his medals that were awarded to him for his bravery and extreme acts of heroic deeds, meaning bravery, valiant, and a courages hero, all together my eternal grandfather who was awarded five bravery medals: The GC VC DSO DSM CBE was lying in Hospital and dying and that he told his wife my grandma my mothers mother who told my mother that he will not die happy until he could see me his best grandson as he has something very important that he wants me to promise him that I will do for him so I decided that because of the terrible sad and tragic news that my mother told me over the telephone that my maternal grandfather is seriously ill and dying in Hospital and shall not die happy until he see's me after all if it had not been for my eternal grandfather who with the help of an MP who at that time was an (MP) for the county and the vast large country side of Lancashire the UK who helped us to escape from this foreign country a country in East-Central Europe, in the year of 1950 I would not be here and alive to write this Fact-based Events true story in this book, I explained to my beautiful dearest lovely future wife and her mother and father and their family that my hero my maternal grandfather was critically ill and dying in hospital and he will not die happy until he see's me his favourate grandson, I told my future wife and her mother father and there family its because of my maternal grandfather who saved myself and his daughter and her young children from certain death, that I would never have have met meaning meet their beautiful daughter who I am looking forward to getting married to on the

26th of October 1968 and spending the rest of both our lives together they understood me and were very sorry to hear the tragic and really sad news about my Hero maternal grandfather lying in a Hospital located somewhere in the county and the vast enormous large country side of Lancashire the UK close to dying they understood the sadness that I must be feeling has with out his help to get is English daughter my English mother and her English born young children back home to there country of the UK alive and safe from this small one room cold damp freezing rat infested drafty old wash room cellar in this village located somewhere in the vast enormous extremely large country of Poland a large country in East–Central Europe, I explained to my wife to be parents her mother and her father that it was only through the strenous effert of my maternal grandfather a world war one Hero and a local MP who at that time was an MP for the county and the large enormous large country side of Lancashire the UK that I am alive and well and that I am truly looking forward to marrying their beautiful daughter, I told them that I will return back with my family from the county and country of Lancashire in the early hours of the morning around about 6 to 7 am on the 26th of October 1968 So with that I made plans to drive two days before my wedding day on the 26th October 1968 on the 24th October 1968 over night to my home town located somewhere in the busy county and country side of Lancashire north west the UK To see and be with my family and my best friend in the whole wide world my maternal hero grandfather who was seriously ill and close to dying from his world war one war wounds he received as a stretcher bearer on the battle field during the course of world war one, It saddens and grieves me so much to that my maternal hero grandfather who sadly and most tragically passed away and died from his war wounds one day the 25th October 1968 before our wedding won't be attending myself and my future wife's wedding day on the 26th October 1968, it realy was a tragic sad and heart breaking moment in my life for me personally it upset me badly knowing that my brave eternal world war one Hero my maternal grandfather would not be attending at myself and my future wife's wedding day on the 26th October 1968, which will be taking place in the scenic picturesque beautiful and charming country side large farming villages local church based somewhere in the county and the vast large area of the country side of Wiltshire, After the sad and tragic death of my maternal grandfather on the 25th October 1968, I returned back to this R.A.F. Transport Command Station were I was stationed and serving at based somewhere in the picturesque charming and beautiful Wiltshire country side and the large farming village in the county of Wiltshire a country in the vast enormous and large country of Wiltshire the UK, with my family from the county and the vast enormously large country side of Lancashire the UK following me in there cars to the scenic beautiful picturesque country side large farming village were my future wife and her parents lived in the county and vast large picturesque scenic country side of Wiltshire for myself and my soon to be future wife's wedding day on the 26th October 1968 as I was driving my car back along the dark night time south bound motorways left hand third lane (Lane One) with my family following behind me in there own cars, I was feeling so exhausted and tired as I did not have any proper sleep for nearly 24 hours that I fell asleep at the wheel of my car I was driving, but luck was with me has my car veared to the left onto the motoway's south-bound left hand 3rd lanes hard shoulder, I was suddenly awakened by the noise of my car tires running over the hard shoulders gravel which was lucky for me as the sound of my car tyres running over the hard shoulder's gravel woke me up and I reacted quickly and I got hold of my cars steering wheel and I quickly changed down from gear no 4 to the lowest gear no 1 to help slow my car down slowly and pushed down gentle on my cars brake peddle to bring my car to a gentle stop on the south bound motorways third lane left hand hard shoulder other wise it could have been a lot more fatal such as my car changing direction abruptly and possible flipping over on to its roof and possible causing me fatal injury or even death luckily it the south bound motorway was quite and there was hardly any traffic movement on the south-bound motorway, once again I came close to the brink of death and walked away from it, After a little while I pulled myself together after my step-father give me a little whiskey to help me keep awake and carry on driving my car to Wiltshire which it did help after driving for an hour on the motorway we finally reached the motorway which will lead myself and my family following me too our destination the picturesque scenic charming photographic country side road of Wiltshire after we depart from this motorway it should only take about 45 minutes to drive to this pictuesque and charming Wiltshire country side large farming village were my soon to be future wife and her family lives, and were this Transport Command R.A.F. Station were I am stationed and serving at is based, After about 45 minutes of driving we finally reached this large farming village and the farming village house were my future wife and her family would be waiting for us to arrive, as we were all getting out of our cars at my soon to be wife's parents house my soon to be beautiful wife and her family came running out of the house to greet us all I introduced my family to my soon to be wife's parents her mother and father, after the introduction we all went into my soon to be wife's mother and fathers house for a cup of tea after having the cup of tea I looked at my watch and the time was 7.15 am I told my soon to be wife that I must go to the caravan that I have rented to get myself ready for our wedding and return to take my parents to our rented caravan based on this caravan site so that they could get themselves ready for our wedding at 100 hours military time noun (1pm) today the 26th of October 1968, I explained to my family and my futur wifes parents that I am only renting this caravan until I am allocated

R.A.F. married quarters, the caravan site was only about 1 mile away in distance from the country side farming village, and the R.A.F. Station that I was stationed and serving at, And also my soon to be future wifes parents family home and the church which were both based just outside of this Transport Command's R.A.F. Station, and also my soon to be wife's family house and the villages church were myself and my beautiful future wife were to be married at on the 26th October 1968 at this church which was based just outside of this R.A.F. Transport Command Station's compound meaning it is an enclosed area of land that is attached to this R.A.F, Transport Command Station, Our wedding day which is to take place on the 26 October 1968 turned out to be a magical warm and sunny day, the beautiful smile on her face I shall always treasure and hold deap with in my very heart for the rest of my eternal life and a day that shall shine on in my broken heart for every and all of eternity It was so very difficult for me to believe that 35 years later on that my dearest beautiful Wife who I met noun meet in this picturesque scenic charming large farming village location somewhere in the vast enormous large area of the country side of Wiltshire the UK that all I have got left of her is my memories of when I first met noun meet my future wife in 1966 in this R.A.F. Transport Command station's military service personal's club based in this R.A.F. Station based in this large farming village, I remember when I first met noun meet my future wife she worked at a food factory located somewhere in this beautiful town steeped in history in the heart of Wiltshire a county and country in the UK, also it was only about 5 miles or more from this R.A.F. Transport Command Station which I was stationed and serving at and also were my dearest late deceased wife lived with her family a couple of yards away from the main entrance gates of this R.A.F. Transport command Station where I was stationed and serving at based in this picturesque beautiful charming scenic village and the church were myself and my late tragically deceased beautiful future wife were to be married in on the 26th October 1968 our wedding day was a fantastic and magical occasion in my life the sun was shining it all went well except for one thing that was missing on that special day in my life and that was my world war one hero my maternal grandfather was not with us at my wedding, I was really looking forward for my maternal grandfather to be present at our wedding but unfortunately he died tragically in Hospital from his world war one war wounds on the 25 October 1968 one day before our wedding day on the 26 October 1968, what was sad and so tragic about it was the fact that I remember my maternal grandfather saying to me that one day in your life when you are grown up in the near future you will meet a beautiful young girl and you will marry her and when that days comes I want you to invite me to your wedding, I assured him that I shall not only invite him to our wedding I also want him to be my best man wearing his world war one medals at our wedding as it will make myself and my soon to be beautiful wife very proud to have him as best man especially wearing his medal's, at our wedding, It sadden's and grieves me emotionally that my maternal grandfather could not be at our wedding I miss him so very much because with out him I would not be alive here in my country the UK to write my Fact-based events true story in this book Title From the Brink of Death and the Gates of Hell, fills me and whats left of my broken heart with lots of emotions, but I must persist and continue on as I have a mission to complete and that mission is to write and finish this Fact-based events true story in this book so that my maternal grandfathers tragic death shall not be in vain, to continue on with my story about the wedding, after our wedding we went on our honeymoon to stay in a hotel which I had already booked for us before our wedding in this seaside coastal town based somewhere in the vast large and enormous area and country side of north-west Lancashire the UK, to celebrate our marriage for two weeks after enjoying ourselves as a newly married couple for two weeks in this hotel in this seaside resort coastal town of north-west Lancashire the UK, in 1968 I drove myself and my new wife in my 1950s saloon car to stay for a week with my parents and family in their home town where I was born and bred on the 20th July 1943 in this busy seaside resorts north-coast county town based somewhere in the vast enormous and extremely large country of Lancashire the UK, after a week we returned back to the large farming village were my new wife's parents and family lived and also were this R.A.F. Transport Command Station was based where I was stationed and serving at based somewhere in the vast enormous and exstremely large country side of Wiltshire a country in the UK, after we returned back to the county and country side of Wiltshire a county in the UK my beautiful new wife left her job at this food factory she worked at in this town steeped in history and heritage to work for the R.A.F. as a civilian cleaner cleaning the R.A.F. Station transport commands married officers families houses situated just across the road from this R.A.F. transport command station's main entrance gates, For the next three years my dear wife was very happy working for the R.A.F. transport command station as a civilian cleaner, and we were both very happy being married we had some good times together while I was stationed at this R.A.F. transport command station based somewhere in the large country of Wiltshire the UK, that was until one day I had an appiontment to see the R.A.F. station's Commanding Officer who told me that I was being posted to this other R.A.F. station based somewhere in south-east of the UK, because of my health and injury I could not do my full duties and could only work for a few hours a day which in military terms means light duties and also because I have only one year left to serve in the R.A.F. of my nine years service R.A.F. Abingdon was the only other option left being a much smaller R.A.F. Station, The only other option would have been a medical discharge from this very busy R.A.F. transport command station where every military service personal have full time day and night time shift work responsibilities, I agreed with him and accepted my posting to this R.A.F. Station Abingdon based somewhere in south-east of the UK, It was to be my finnal and last posting on active service in the R.A.F. as I have only one year left to serve in the R.A.F. before I retire from active services duties in the R.A.F. back into civi street and civilian life, I shall miss serving on active service in the R.A.F. very much even though I have faced death in the face and came close to the Brink of Death on several occasions but survived as I have a mission to complete after I retire back into civi street and civillian life through an injury I received while serving in the R.A.F. my whole life and my ambition was to serve on active service in the Armed Military Forces Services the R.A.F. for our Queen and her Royal Family, and to sustain the freedom for the people of the UK, in the R.A.F. until I was too old to serve any longer in the R.A.F. but because of my injury and ill health I could not resign on for further service in the R.A.F. which made me feel very sad and unhappy but life must go on and forward,

[[THE YEAR WAS 1972]]

After my honourable discharge in the year of 1972 from the R.A.F. after nine years plus three years reserve service total 12+ years meritorious – exemplary service in the armed military forces the R.A.F. myself and my wife moved back to my home town of the busy northen seacoast town of Lancashire the UK, My dear and beautiful wife was pregnant at the time and as I was driving along this northbound carriage of this motorways third lane (Lane One) a 1960s car that was in front of me about two car length away was moving really slow along this north-bound carriage motorways third lane (Lane One) so I decided to over take this car as the driver of this 1960s car was only doing about 40 miles an hour along this north-bound carriage motorways third lane (Lane One) so I decided to moved over to the middle second lane (Lane Two) to over take this car driver which I did with no problems but I could not believe it as the driver of this 1960s car suddenly raced past me at a very fast speed he must have be doing at least 90 miles an hour along this north-bound carriage motorways overtaking lane (Lane One) known to most car drivers as the fast lane, of this motorway, I looked at my dear pregnant wife and said to her that I have this strange feeling that this driver is going to end up in a really serious accident somewhere along this north-bound carriage of this motorway, I told her not to worry as this motorways next service station and restaurant is less than a mile away and it should only take us about 15 to 10 minutes to drive to this service station and restaurant to have a rest and something to eat and drink especially after driving all day long and over night from the country of Wiltshire, also this service station was not far from this other and much shorter in distance motorway, which is only 15.4 miles travel time and it will only take 16 minutes driving time along this north-bound motorway to this exit turn off onto this other and final north-bound motorway and once on this north-bound motorway it will only take about 20 minutes driving time as its only 3.4 miles to drive to this busy northern seaside coastal town of north-west Lancashire the UK, to continue about myself and my pregnant wife's long journey along this major north-bound carriage of this motorway and this stupid and reckless and careless mad driver who I said to my dear pregnant wife that this driver is going to end up in a serious accident somewhere along this north-bound carriage of this motorway, my wife looked worried so I told my dear pregnant wife don't worry about this stupid driver as it won't be long now before we reach this turn of exit that will lead us on to this north-bound motorways service station and restaurant were we can rest and have a drink and something to eat, so we won't see this stupid speeding car driver being involved in an accident, so I thought but the worst-case scenario situation nightmare that any one could imagine was about to happen as a disaster was just a few minutes away because as I was slowing down to drive my car across from this north-bound carriage motorways middle Lane (Lane 2) onto this north-bound carriage motorways left hand third Lane (Lane 1) I suddenly noticed that in my cars front head lights beam something lying on this north-bound carriage motorways middle Lane [Lane 2] but before I could do any thing my car hit this thing lying in the north-bound carriage motorways middle lane (Lane 2) there was such a loud noise as I my car hit this thing it caused my car to vear and swerve sharply and dangerously from this north-bound carriage motorways middle lane (lane 2) to the left hand north-bound carriage motorways third lane (Lane One) of this north-bound motorway and vear of course on to the hard shoulder and heading dangerously toward a large HGV heavy goods truck that was parked on the hard shoulder just a few yards away from this over turned car which was lying on its roof with the car drivers door open and the car engine still running lying on this motorways left hand carriageways north-bound hard shoulder, Luckily my long driving experience came in really handy as I just managed to miss it by a few inches and pull to a stop on this north-bound carriage motorways hard shoulder just a few yards away from the HGV 'heavy goods truck on the hard shoulder another inch and I would have hit the parked heavy good's truck left hand side possible causing serous injury to myself and my pregnant wife which in most serious accidents could have resulted in death, eventually the motorway police and the emergency services arrived as the lorry driver had already phoned them but did not stay to explain to them what had happened, he told me that he had to leave because he as a urgent early morning delivery to deliver in the lake district, any how when the motorway police emergency accident unit arrived to close off the north-bound carriage of this motorway, they shone the police vehicals spot light on to this north-bound carriage motorways second middle Lane (Lane 2) which was less then half mile away in distance from this north-bound carriage motorways service station and restaurant, I could now see what I had run over on this north-bound carriage middle lane (Lane 2) of this motorway it was a terrible horrific and gastly sight to see as what I saw was a torso definition a human body without a head arms or legs lying in whats left of this body in this north-bound carriage motoways middle lane (Lane 2) of this north-bound carriage motorway which was run over many times by heavy goods vehicals and once by my car after a short while a motorway police officer approached and asked me were the HGV heavy good's lorry driver was I told him that he told me that he had an emergency early morning delivery to do somewhere in the vast large country of Lancashire the UK, he then asked me if myself and my wife were ok I said yes just feeling a bit shaken up but my wife is pregnant but I think she is ok and that we both need to take a rest and something to drink and eat as I have been driving all of the way from the country side of Wiltshire yesterday and over night and it is my long driving experience and my quick reaction that I avoided hitting by a few inches this HGV heavy goods vehicle. The motorway police officer asked me if I new what I had hit and run over on the middle Lane (Lane 2) of this north bound motorway I replied yes I think so as I had a torch which I pointed at what my car had hit and run over on the middle Lane (Lane 2) of this north bound carriage motorway, what I saw at first glance in the beam of this torch I was not to sure at first what it was but then after another look I think it was part of the remains of the body of the car driver of this car which was lying up side down on its roof on this north-bound carriage of this motorway's hard shoulder, I explained to this police motorway patrol officer that this car lying on its roof on the hard shoulder looked like the one that went speeding passed me along this north-bound carriage motorway's first lane (Lane 1) at a really fast speed and swerving a little from side to side I told him that I said to my pregnant wife that this idiot and stupid car driver is bound to end up in a serious car accident some where along this north-bound carriage of this motorway, this motorway police officer thanked me for this important information as it should help him in his enquiries regarding this terrible and tragic car accident the north-bound motorway traffic police officer asked me to follow him to this motorways police station just a few yards away from this motorways service station and restaurant he looked at me and told me not too worry as he is not going to arrest me as its only just to see if my car is road worthy and also to see if there are any human remains attached to the under neath of my car so that they can wash and clean any human remains from underneath my car with a power water jet hosepipe, I assured this motorway patrol police officer that my car is 100% road worthy as the week before my car was in a garage having new brake pad discs and four new car tyres fitted and the car engine given a full service, is reply was thats ok and as I have already told you it just to make sure that any human remains attached to any part your cars body are removed and cleaned off your car, my reply was ok and I followed the police patrol vehical to this north-bound motorways police station situated only a few yards away from this car park and restaurant of the motoways north bound service station, once we arrived at the motorways police station I handed my car keys to this motorways traffic police officer who had brought two cups of tea for myself and my pregnant wife he told us to relax and if we wanted to we could have a cigarette has he was about to leave he told me that he won't be long and shall return in about half an hour with my car keys so with that he left us alone, after about half an hour he returned and told me that he would like a word with me on my own about my car I looked at my pregnant wife and told her not to worry I shall return in a couple of minutes the police officer also said to her don't worry love its nothing to worry about your husband will be with you very soon its just show him that his car as been cleaned thats all then you can both go and park the car on the car park as its been a long night for both of you driving all the way from Wiltshire you need to get something to drink and eat before you continue on with your journey with that I stepped out side of the police waiting room with the traffic police officer who once out side told me this he said I needed to talk to you on your own has I did not want your pregnant wife to hear what I am about to tell you see the forensic team police officer found part of what was left of this persons head and his or her brain stuck under neath the cars front wheels and suspension, which connects your car vehicle's system of tyres, springs, and the cars shock absorbers that connects a vehicle to it wheels, the forensic team has washed all of what was left of the humand remains you run over on the north-bound carriage motorway's middle lane (Lane Two) with a powerful hosepipe water jet, which is now cleaned off all of the human remains that your car run-over on the north-bound carriage motorways middle lane (Lane 2) from under neath your car, a deadly thought came to mind that once again I had faced death and I came really close to the brink of death and the gates hell, and survived it, to continue the motoway traffic patrol police man handed me back my car keys and we went back into the motorways police stations waiting room were my pregnant wife was waiting he told her that everything is ok and that we can continue on with our journey after we have had something to eat in the service stations resturant which we did as we were both starving and needed something to eat, after myself and my wife finished eating our meal in the service stations restaurant we continued on with our journey to were I was born and bred on the 20th July 1943 in the north-west busy seaside resorts fylde coastal town of North-west Lancashire the UK, To start a new career back in civilian life, After myself and my wife settled in my home town of this busy northern seaside resort coastal county town of north-west Lancashire the UK, I began working as a manual worker at a chemical works based somewhere in the county and country of northwest Lancashire the UK, which at first I enjoyed working at this chemical works it was very interesting work but also a could be a dangerous and risky Job meaning the chance of loss of life or serious injury leading to possible death when cleaning certain types of machinery, I only worked at this chemical works for nine months because the chemicals in this chemical works started to affect my duodenal ulcer which made me feel ill, I had to finish working at this chemical works because of my duodenal ulcer which was affected by the chemicals,

[[THE YEAR WAS 1972 AND MY NEW LIFE BACK IN CIVI STREET]]

To continue from above after leaving my job at the chemicals works I went with my wife to this busy coastal towns local job center to look for another job after awail I came across a vacancy advertisement advertising for a bus conductor and a fully qualified PSV public service vehical bus driver, I looked at my dear beautiful wife said to her that I am going to apply for that position as a bus conductor her reply was quite positive so with that I applied for this position as a bus conductor which I was successful and secured this job, so my new life and my second job in civillian life began as a trainee bus conductor working for this bus and tram transport company based somewhere in this northern busy seaside resorts fylde coastal town of North-west Lancasire the UK, My first day with other new trainee bus conductors at this bus and tram depot was first of all to learn how to use these old bus conductors ticket tim-machines during the course of the first day this depots inspector who was teaching us told us that tomorrow morning some of you shall be working on either a bus or a tram as a conductor with a qualified bus or tram conductor for a week to learn all of the buses and trams routes, the after a week you shall start your normal duties as either a bus or tram conductor, luckily my job position was a bus conductor which I did for a full year after a full year working as a bus conductor I was told by this depots chief bus inspector that as from tomorrow morning you will be taken of bus conductors duties and start with one of this depots fully qualified PSV buses driving instructor who will be learning and teaching you to drive this depots old double-decker bus drivers learner training vehical for three weeks after three weeks if the PSV driving instructor thinks you are good enough he will forward an application form for you to take your PSV public service vehical drivers licence test which should only take about half and hour to complete your PSV driving test, and if you pass your PSV public service vehical driving test you will receive your PSV bus drivers red lapel badge and your PSV bus drivers full licence in about a week until then you will return to your normal duties as a bus conductor, which I did and after a week I did received my PSV red lapel drivers badge and my PSV full bus drivers Licence, To cut a long story short I worked on the buses as a PSV public service vehical bus driver and conductor for nearly thirteen years and during the thirteen years I worked a lot of overtime on either a tram or a bus as a conductor most of the time working one hundreds hours a week during this really busy seaside resorts towns holiday summer season's but during the course of my thirteen years service as a bus driver conductor it was not without its near close encounter incidents, such as on one occasion while I was working overtime as a bus conductor on this double-decker bus that was stopped just across the road from this towns busy bus station the driver had to go to this bus stations staffs toilets to relieve him self, it was while I was standing on the double-deckers passengers access platform that there was such a loud bang sounding like a bomb had just dropped pushing me forward away from the rear end of this double-decker bus knocking me of balance it was when I pulled myself together I noticed these trucks two fork-lift-forks sticking through the rear-end of this double-decker buses passengers access platform on either side of both my right and left leg, All I know is the fact that if I had been standing another inch to the left hand side of this double-decker buses rear-end passengers access platform that these trucks two fork-lift-forks would have definitely hit and possible crushed both of my left and right legs causing sever injury which results in either death or long-term disability, But I was so lucky this time and survived the impact that could have caused my death, once again I had faced death in the face and walked away from it but for how long only time will tell in the long run, anyway to continue on about these trucks two fork-lift-forks, I could not at first believe what I was looking at as when I got of the bus I could see that this large truck with these two fork-lift-forks had crashed into the rear-end of this double-decker bus that I was conducting on, what gets me is how in Hells name did the driver of this large truck with these two fork-lift-forks sticking at the front of his truck not see this large double-decker bus stopped at this passengers bus-stop I suppose it was through the lack of concentration, this was only one of the many near death close encounter incidents that I had while I was working on the buses for nearly thirteen years, It was through these many long and tiring hours working one hundreds hours a week on the buses and these many near close encounter incidents that I decided after 13 years working on the buses as a PSV bus driver and conductor that with much sorrow I decided to hand in a months notice too be able if possible find a job driving what ever with less hours not only that so that I could spend more time with my wife and our not to long born baby-boy, after my months notice was over I finished my job working on the buses,

[[THE YEAR WAS 1984 AND ONCE AGAIN I WAS CLOSE TO THE BRINK OF DEATH AS WRITTEN IN THIS FOLLOWING STORY BELOW]]

To continue from above I went to the Job center and soon found another driving job position that was advertised in this job center looking for a qualified PSV coach driver it sounded interesting so I applied for this vacancy position that was advertised in this local job center for an experienced coach driver who holds a fully endorsed PSV licence, to work as a full time coach driver for this private hire coach company based somewhere in the vast large county and country of Lancashire the UK, I had no problem in getting this job because of my vast experience working for 13 years on the buses as a qualified approved PSV public service vehical bus driver, it was a good job at the beginning it went quite well I was driving and taking school children in the private hire luxury coach to different venues every week in the vast large surrounding area of the county and country of Lancashire the UK, That was until one day I was asked by the person who owned this private hire luxury coach company to well there was no problems with the couch, that pick up and collect about eighty young school children and their school teachers from a school located somewhere in this industrial town based somewhere in the country of north-west Lancashire the UK, at 6 AM in the early hours of the next morning and drive them for 5 hours & 20 minutes in distance 300.07 square miles in which I could not believe was a 10 wheeled old 1940s coach which at the time I did not know that it faulty brakes to this major ferry seaport located in this industrial town location somewhere in this country in the south-east of the UK and get them there in time to catch a ferry which I did arrive in plenty of time for them to catch this ferry, the long tiring 5 hour and 20 minutes journey to this south-east port went was until the long tiring drive back return journey which once again would take 5 hours and 20 minutes in distance 300,07 square miles back to my home town located somewhere in the country of Lancashire the UK, as I was driving this 10 wheeled 1940s old coach through this real busy large famous city, which took along time for me to drive through it, as there was so much traffic that it was the case of having to use the coaches brake's quite a lot it was when I was half way through the city that the worse case scenario happened its was when I had to brake hard using the coaches brakes to help me stop because the car in front of me suddenly braked hard to avoid hitting a cyclist who nearly fell of his bike, To continue, to my horror the coaches brakes were no working as they should do and that the worst-case Scenario could happen if I did not act quickly I could end up crashing into this car in front who had suddenly braked hard to try and avoid hitting a cyclist, I got hold of the coaches gear stick and changed down from gear 4 to gear 3 and then to gear 2 and lastly gear 1, A method and technique that I learned while serving as a civilian volunteer reserve in the TA Territorial Army learning to drive various army Vehicals before I joined the R.A.F. To continue the reason being that you can also use a vehicals gears as an emergency braking system if your vehicals brakes fail by working together quickly with both the vehicals gear-stick and clutch, by by changing the coaches gears down from 4 to 1 together with the vehicals clutch by bringing the clutch up gently with your left foot, thus; therefore bringing the coach to a stop luckily there was no vehicals close to the coaches rear-end, once again I nearly came too close, to the brink of death, but luck was on my side and I once again cheated the brink of death and the gates of hell, To continue, after the near and close incident I continued with my journey through this busy city which I managed to with no further incident to drive and get this old coach safely through this famous large city which luckily

I did then I continued on with my journey driving this old 10 wheeler 1940s coach to connect with this vast long busy north-bound motorway that in distance stretches thousand and thousands of square miles, Once I had connected with this busy north-bound motorway I must not forget that this coach had no brakes to slow it down a little and to stop it in case of an emergency such as a major accident, so in that case I had would have to think quickly and be prepared for the worse case scenario to happen as I was driving this brakeless old 1940s ten wheeler coach along this busy north-bound motorway carriage first lane (Lane One) which is close to the north-bound carriage lanes hard shoulder, Luckily the coach was now empty which help to make the coach a lot lighter in weight, and there was away that I could slow and stop the coach and that was by using the coaches gears and clutch together, It was a really tough and long dangerous journey driving this 10 wheeled old 1940s coach with no brakes along this north-bound first lane (Lane One) carriage of this motorway late at night, luckily with hardly any traffic traveling on this north-bound carriage of this motorway, That will lead me eventually towards this other shorter in distance north-bound motorway's exit turn off that will take me about 2 hours and 59 minutes to get there as its 12.2 square mile to get there and hopeful safely with no further incidents happening on this north-bound carriage motorway that stretches in distance thousand and thousand's of square miles, Luckly I was not traveling along way in distance on this motorways north-bound carriageway, Only a short distance Re; 12.2 square miles along this motorway to this exit turn off location that will lead me onto this other home ward bound north-bound motorway, and once there it should only take me about half an hour to reach my native home town of this busy northern seaside resort and coastal county town were I was born and bred on the 20th July 1943 in north-west Lancashire the UK, After a peaceful but tiring journey with no further major incidents happening along this shorter motorway as it was virtually empty of any traffic, I finally arrived safely in my native northern seaside resort county town and country of north-west Lancashire the UK, after a short drive driving this 10 wheeled old 1940s coach with hardly any brakes to help to stop this coach only the coaches gears I arrived at this petrol stations forecourt noun an open area in front or behind a petrol station were this coach company parked its coaches, once there I finally parked the coach, I could not believe that I had made it back safely, The next day I return back to this garage were I had parked the coach, I noticed this mechanic looking at the coach I approached him and asked him what he was doing he looked at me and said that I have been asked by the coaches company to inspect this coach to see if there was any damage done I looked at him and asked him have you inspected the coaches braking system he replied not as yet, I looked at him and told him that he had better check this coaches brakes as they are not working I had to drive this old 1940s ten-wheeler coach along the motoway with hardly any brakes to stop me in an emergency on this motorway luckily I managed to drive this old 1940s ten-wheeler coach for over three hours along two different really busy motorways from one end of the country back to this garage here in Lancashire the UK, as far as I can see that this coaches braking system as never been checked and serviced for quite sometime, they were working ok at the time that I was driving this old coach with these young school children and their school teachers, to this major ferry seaport located somewhere in this Industrial town in the South-east of the UK, It was on the return journey when things went wrong, I decided that I have had enough of driving and working for this coach company so I left this Job and decided that I have had enough and that because of my health reasons I shall retire which my GP told me to do a long time ago,

[[THE TRAGIC YEAR WAS 2001 AND UNBELIEVABLE I WAS ONCE AGAIN FACING DEATH IN THE FACE AS WRITTEN IN THE FOLLOWING STORY BELOW]]

It as to be said that in all of the near close encounters of a near close to death situation this was the most serious and really frighting one that I had experienced even so it could be said that I once again had cheated the brink of death and the Gates of Hell. But unbelievable and beyond belief once again this evil death wish curse was still stalking me, I have tried time and time again to try and break free from this evil death wish curse but once again and most sadly and tragically this time I am facing death, in the most up setting and heart braking way possible the tragic and untimely and sudden unexpected passing and death of my beautiful princess my dearest beautiful wife who was diagnosed with cancer by our local GP Doctor who I had telephoned and explained to him that my wife was seriously ill and is suffering with severe pains in her stomach so much that I am really concerned about her he replied ok I am on my way and shall be with you shortly when he arrived he examined my dear beautiful wife's stomach and her temperature which he told me was high, he looked at me and said that he needs to have a word with me in private, I replied ok and asked him to follow me to the kitchen were upon he said to me I think you already have an idea what your wife is really seriously ill with I replied to him yes I do recognise the symptoms they are the same symptoms that both my dearest late deceased brave and courages English Mother and my late deceased wife's late deceased Mother both who suffered and sadly passed away and tragically died of terminal cancer, I had this terrible feeling that my dear wife is suffering with this terrible illness Cancer he replied yes she is and your wife needs most urgently to be admitted as an emergency into Hospital so as to have an Xray taken ASAP to show how bad her cancer is and how far it as spread through out her body I stood there for a few seconds he asked me if I was ok I replied not really but I shall pull myself together and take my wife to this Hospital in my car now instead of her being rushed there in an emergency ambulance has that will really upset and frighten her so very much he replied ok can I use your phone to phone this Hospital's ward 9 and inform them that you are bringing your wife to this Hospital's ward 9 for urgent medical tests and an X- ray, who after checking her has the symptons of having cancer, when I arrived with my wife at this Hospitals Ward 9 the wards sister and nursing staff had already prepared a bed for my late wife as they need to urgently get my late wife ready to have an X- ray, I looked at my beautiful wonderful darling wife who though she was in great pain smiled at me I told her that I will return and be with you tomorrow morning but firstly I will be going to see and help my brother first thing in then morning as soon as I have finished making sure that my dear brother is ok I will then make my way to the Hospital's ward 9 to visit and especially to see and be with you my dear wife she looked at me with her beautiful tearful blue eyes and radiant smile in which I tried really hard not show my tears and emotions in front of her, I said ok my love I look forward to seeing you tomorrow morning and hopefully be able to come home with you I told my dear beautiful wife don't you worry darling I will make quite sure that you will return back with me to our home tomorrow you just for today rest and try to get your self better I love you and only you, you are my most very special beautiful princess I treasure every passing moment with of I think of you always because you bloom like a red rose deap with in my heart, so as the story goes I said good bye to my wife and got into my car and made my way home, my son was at home he asked me were is mother I told him that she was not feeling well so our doctor made arrangements with Hospital's ward 9 to admit your mother as an emergency in patent to have an X- Ray taken of your mother condition my son looked worried I told him that everything shall turn out ok with your mother, even though deep with in my heart and my feelings I knew what I told my son was not true but until the results of my dearest wife's X-Ray is looked at by the hospitals doctor's I had to keep my son in the dark so as too not worry him to much, early the very next morning I drove my car to visit and see if my brother as ok and if there was anything he needed from the shop he used to go to around the corner from his flat on when I walked into his flat his two best friends were there with him and they had already been to the shop for my brother as he did not know if I was able to visit him with my wife being seriously ill, he asked me how was I explained to him that she had got worse and I had to call our doctor's surgery and told them that I have an emergency with my wife she is really seriously ill and I need my family Dr to come and see her most urgently 'ASAP' which he did after checking my wifes condition he looked at me and said I think that you have an idea what your wife is suffering with I said yes I do and that I had a very good idea that my wife was suffering with that fateful virus disease cancer our doctor more or less confirmed that it was cancer that my dearest wife is suffering with but to be sure the doctor asked me if he could use my telephone to phone the Hospitals ward 9 so as to have my wife admitted for further tests, after talking to a doctor of ward 9 to have my wife admitted for further tests he told me that rather then wait for an emergency ambulance to take her to hospital, would it be possible for you to take your wife straight away in your car to ward 9 at this Hospital I said yes I will he still had my house phone in his hand and spoke to the doctor of ward 9 and I heard him tell the doctor that the patients husband is bringing her to ward 9 now and shall arrive there within a few minutes, I already had packed in a carrier bag most of the things my wife shall need whilst she is in hospital, our doctor helped to take my wife to my car and told me that he shall be in contact with me once he gets the medical report from the Hospital, with that I drove my wife straight away to the hospital and once there took my wife to ward 9 were the staff nurse and another nurse was waiting to take my wife to the wards bed, were she is now waiting to have an X-ray I kissed her good bye and told her that I will visit her later today and for her not to worry and that I love her so very much and also she will get better medical attention here on ward 9 than she would at home,

[[THE YEAR WAS 2001 AND ONCE AGAIN I AM FACING DEATH IN THE FACE AS WRITTEN IN THE FOLLOWING STORY BELOW]]

To continue from above with that I left her and returned back home to let my son know that is mother is in the Hospital on ward 9 and that I will find out today when I go to see and visit on ward 9 if the X-ray as confirmed that my dearest wife has got cancer just as I said that I received a phone call on my mobile phone it was from the senior staff nurse of ward 9 who asked me if I could come immediately to ward 9 as your wife as received some bad news from the doctor of ward 9 who is talking to her now at her bedside I told the senior staff nurse that I am on my way now I should be there in about ten minutes please tell my wife that I will be with her very soon, for a moment I just stood there I had a job to speak as my worsed fears about my wife having cancer was confirmed I looked at my brother and his two friends and told them that I have to rush to see and be with my wife on ward 9 as the phone call that I have just received on my mobile phone is from the senior staff nurse of ward 9 advised me that my wife as been told by the hospital's ward 9 Hospital doctor who is at the moment speaking to your wife at her hospital bedside on ward 9 that her X-ray came back showing that she as got cancer I could not talk for a few seconds because of this expected but most tragic heart breaking news that she as got Cancer when I could finally talk the Hospital Ward 9 staff nurse told me that your wife is very upset and is crying out for some one to contact me to come and take her home as she does not want to stay in hospital and wants to be with me and her son at home my brother and his two friends looked at me with tears in their eyes my emotions and tears were to hard to control just like they are now while I am writing the heart breaking and most tragic painful unbearable heart-aching story any way to try and continue my brother told me to hurry and go to the hospital brother and be with and find out what the doctors are going to do about my wifes Cancer so with that I drove quite fast to the Hospital once there I immediately made my way to ward 9 as I walked into ward 9 the senior staff nurse was waiting for me with the sister of ward 9 to explain to me about my wifes condition I just told them tell me after I have seen my wife and with that I walked into the ward were my dear wife was lying in bed in tears Seeing my princess my once happy lovely wife in tears broke my heart and it was at that moment that I knew that the heart of my life my lovely most beautiful wife my beautiful princess wouldn't be coming home as I could really see how ill my wife was looking it was so very difficult and hard for me to control me emotions and console myself I had to be brave for the sake of my dear beautiful wife so as not to upset her any more than she already is as I approached her bed she looked at me and got up from her bed and I held her in my arms tightly and kissed her she looked at me and new that I already would have known about her having cancer she looked so ill but still to me she looked so radiant and still was to me the most beautiful looking women in the whole wide world anyway my wife looked at me and said can we go out side for a cigarette I said to her I do not see any reason why not, so with that I walked with my dearest wife along the ward past the sisters and staff nurses ward 9 office as we were walking past the office a staff nurse came out to see were we where going I told her that my wife wanted to go out side for some fresh air and a cigarette the staff nurse said thats ok but don't be to long as the surgeon doctor wants to have a word with me about your wifes condition I said ok we will be back in about 15 minutes and myself and my wife went out side for some fresh air and a cigarette after a hew minutes out side my dear wife looked at me and said to me that she does not want to die, for a few seconds I did not know what to say to her before I could say anything to my upset dearest most beautiful wife I had first of all try to control my emotions and pull myself together after I had contained my emotions I looked at my wife and said to her don't worry my darling wife I will not let you die I promise you this with all of my heart, I looked at my dearest wife and said to her that you are looking tired so lets get you back up stairs to ward 9 and your bed for you to rest for a few moments while I have a word with the doctor who is looking after you, don't worry to much I will be back with you soon with that I walked along the ward towards the sisters office were the oncololist surgeon noun is a surgeon who has special training in treating cancer)' was waiting to have a word with me about my dear wife cancer He first of all told me that the X-ray had come back and showed that your wife has got cancer, I asked him is there any possibility that you can save my wife with surgery he replied that looking at the X-ray your wife's cancer as spread I remember his words very words that he told me as I do have a really good memory the medical term is metastasis to the liver and lung which until we operate on your wife to find how bad and serious her cancer has spread but until the operation on your wife I can only at this stage tell you that it depends on how far the cancer as spread if its spread to the liver and lungs your wife has a medium life expectancy of less than six months, your wifes prognosis is based on her response to treatment after listening to what the oncololist surgeon had explained to me about my dearest beautiful wife cancer condition and hopefully an operation, I asked the onocolist surgeon when is he going to operate on my wife his answer was in about three weeks time I could not believe what he had just said, my reply to him was is another surgeon going to do the operation on my wife his reply was no I am the only qualified experienced onocolist surgeon who is specially highly trained to do this type of cancer operation in this hospital, I could not believe what I was hearing my wife was seriously ill with cancer and he was going on holiday while my dearest wife was very ill suffering with cancer I took a deap breath and then I asked him if I could take my wife home his reply was yes sir I shall be making arrangements with ward B for your wife to be admitted for further tests and treatment were your wife will be given morphine to help her pain, you can take your wife home for a few days, I asked this hospital onocolist surgeon when will my wife be admitted onto this hospital's ward 9 he replied that your wife should receive a letter from ward 9 for her to be admitted into to the ward I walked across the ward to the bed were my wife was waiting for me I told her that she needs to get ready for me to take her home for a few days until she receives a letter from the Hospital for her to be admitted onto this hospitals ward 9 for more tests and treatment and also be given morphine which is a pain relieving medication to help ease your pain, so I took my wife home it was really heartbreaking for me to watch her suffering in pain from the cancer, she had to sleep down stairs in the lounge on the large sofa as it was so very painful for her to try and climb the stairs to sleep in our bedroom and even go to the toilet so the only conclusion I could see was for my dear beautiful wife to sleep down stairs in the lounge on the large sofa, I also had to try and sleep down stairs in the lounge on an arm chair so I could keep a watch on her just in case she needed my help but after about four days at home my wife pain started to get worse I told our son Paul that his mother as cancer and his waiting for a letter From the Hospitals ward B to arrive to admit her it up set our son Paul I could feel the emotions and pain that he was suffering after all the word Cancer is very hard to bear but finally on the fifth day at home 5th of August 2001 a letter arrived addressed to my wife I opened it and it was from the hospitals ward which is a maternity and also a cancer ward for my dearest wife to be admitted onto this hospitals ward at 10am in the morning on the 5th of August 2001 at 10am I looked at my dear beautiful wife and told her that the letter was from the hospitals Ward for her to be admitted at 10am this morning 5th of August 2001 onto this hospitals ward this hospital for further medical tests and medical treatments, while my beautiful wife was in this hospitals Ward, I visited her every day and at night time to be with her and to try and comfort my darling beautiful wife as she is on a lot of morphine to help ease her cancer pain, if possible I used to take her out side for a cigarette, she was only about four foot eleven in height and believe me when I used to help my wife to get her of the hospital bed it was a bit of a struggle as she was heavy to lift of the hospital bed as the cancer made her stomach look like she was pregnant, as the days passed there still was no news from the hospitals doctors regarding operating on my wife to see how bad the cancer was, I asked one of the ward staff nurses when are the doctors going to do this operation, regarding my wifes cancer this hospitals ward staff nurse reply was that she will go and see the matron in charge of this hospitals ward to find out if there is any news about your wife, awaile later she returned and told me that the matron in charge of this hospitals ward told her that the qualified and experienced onocolist surgeon will be operating on my wife sometime next week and that he shall be coming to see her in about five minutes to talk to her about the operation procedure next week, after about five minutes he came to see my wife and myself and explained to my wife and me about the operation he will be doing on my wife next week, after he finished

talking about my wifes operation next week 'date 11th August 2001
he looked at me and said if its ok with you your wife if she wishes
can go home for a few days, until next week, my dearest wife did
not know what to say to this hospital onocolist surgeon as she was
on morphine to help ease the cancer pain I asked him do you think
its ok for my wife to come home with me as it would be more than
great for me and my son but look at her she is confused because of
the affects of the morphine and what makes you think that it will
be ok for my wife to go home for a week and then return back to
the hospital's ward next week on the 11th August 2001 to have this
operation to see how bad her cancer is he looked at me and before
he could say anything I told him that I would like a word with him
in private with that we both left the wards bed room that my wife
was lying in seriously ill suffering from cancer she was not alone
as her father and her brothers and sisters who had traveled all the
way from this large farming country side village were they lived
location somewhere in the vast enormous large country side of the
county of Wiltshire the UK to visit my dear wife there eldest sister
and stay by her bedside in this hospitals ward for awile, once out
side of the bedroom I looked at this hospital doctor and said to him
in these word look I am no doctor but I do know all about the
effects and the symptoms of this terrible decease cancer as my
mother suffered for five years with terminal cancer which she died
tragically from, also my wife;s mother, my mother-in-law was ill
and dying with cancer and tragically passed away and also died in
this hospital were she was a patient in located somewhere in this
country side Wiltshire town from terminal cancer, and I do know
and have this terrible feeling that if you allow my wife to go home
she won't survive with out proper nursing care attention and
medication such as morphine which if given to much morphine
could kill her she needs proper medical help and attention from
qualified trained nurses, were as being at home my wife will be in

a lot of pain and also the bath room is up a flight of stairs which is more or less impossible for her to climb up with out my help were as here in the hospitals ward my dearest wife will receive the proper medical attention and care so my answer to him was which was painful for me to say was she will be better off staying here in this hospitals ward it was not easy for me to say this to this hospital doctor but he finally agreed that it was the right thing to do, so finally I went back into the bed room to talk to my wife if she could understand me which was so painful for me to tell her that she will be staying in hospital until the operation she said ok darling I understand, I replied ok my dearest beautiful wife, her father and family from Wiltshire the UK looked at me and before they could say anything I told them that it pains and hurts me but its much better for my wife to stay here in hospital where she shall get proper medical attention and morphine to help ease her cancer pain also she will have two of the wards fully qualified trained nurses looking after her and bathing her in the ward's bathroom, it would be impossible for her at home to go to the bathroom as she would have to climb up stairs to use the toilet, I looked at my dearest wife and told her that I will have to leave now to see our son and that myself and our son will be coming to see you this evening, with that I kissed my wife not realizing and knowing at that moment for the last time which brought tear's to my eyes after I left her, I told her not to worry and get some rest with that I left her alone that evening I returned back to the hospitals ward to be with my now seriously ill wife before entering this hospitals ward bedroom that my wife was in I had to compose and pull myself together for a few moments before entering her bedroom as I did not want to show her that I was worried about her having cancer and that for the first time in my life I was not prepared for the eventual tragic death and loss of my long term married partner my beautiful dearest wife and the grief that must follow after all she was my beautiful wife and we have been married for 35 wonderful long happy years and I knew that I could loose her for ever at any moment,

[[THE TRAGIC YEAR WAS 2001 AND DEATH IS FACING ME AS WRITTEN IN THE STORY BELOW]]

To continue from above as I was getting myself ready to drive my eldest brother there I received an urgent call on my mobile phone from the senior staff nurse of this ward were my dearest beautiful wife was a patient in this Hospital wards informing me that my wife had taken a turn for the worse overnight my response was one of complete disbelief m brother and his two friends looked at me with tears in my eyes and knew that something bad had happened I told my brother that I have just had a phone call on my mobile phone from the staff nurse of this hospitals ward informing me that my wife as taken a turn for the worse overnight and that I urgently need to come to the hospitals ward ASAP I told my brother and his two friends that I have this strange feeling that my dear wife has sadly and tragically passed away and has tragically died I don't think I can take you my brother too for your appointment at this SMRC hospital Mobility Limb Center as I have to rush to the hospital's ward to see what's happened to my wife even though I knew that the worse scenario was that my wife had passed away and died, for a moment I looked at both my eldest brother and his two friends who looked stunned by the tragic terrible shocking news about my wife's sudden tragic death did not know what to say to support and comfort me, my brother unbelievably with a little bit of difficulty stood up on his left leg has his right leg below the knee had already been amputated while he was a patient in ward 35 in hospital a year before my dearest beautiful wife was diagnosed with cancer in hospital my dear brother grabbed me by my shoulders and said to me that he and his two friends were really very sorry to hear that my dear wife had died and that there is always another day that we can go to this Limb Center, he said to me that at this specific moment you have a much more important urgent situation to deal with go to the hospital ward beautiful princess my wife who I was married to for over 35 magical and happy years together had passed away and died sadly when I arrived at this hospitals ward I noticed two red cones out side of the bedroom were my wife was a patient as I tried to enter her room the senior ward staff nurse and another ward nurse got hold of me and guided me into the visitors waiting room, I was basically already more or less prepared for what the senior ward staff nurse was about to tell me the tragic news that my wife had passed away and died even though the hospitals ward emergency response team arrived in a matter of seconds there was nothing that they could do to save her even though they tried very hard to revive your wife for a moment I was stunned and lossed for words I just gazed at the visitors waiting room wall I just did not know what to do until the staff nurse asked me if I would like her to call my son to ask him to come to this hospitals ward to see his mother has his mother as taken a turn a turn for the worse I thought for a minute and then I said to the staff nurse yes that will be ok but also can you telephone my two step sisters to let them know that my wife as taken a turn for the worse and would it be possible for them to come to the hospitals ward ASAP I have both there contact numbers in my mobile phone which I handed to the staff nurse and also my brother phone number to let him know that my wife as passed away as he cannot come to see her has I promised to let him know how my wife is the staff nurse said to me that she will go to the sisters office and telephone my family in the mean time I will ask another of ward nurse to come and take you to see your wife I was not ready for what I was about to see as the nurse took me into the room were my dearest beautiful wife was lying in the hospital bed looking so beautiful I just stood there looking at my dearest beautiful wife speechless the Staff nurse left me alone with my wife I just stood there looking at my wife lying there she looked so peaceful like she was asleep I remember saying to her good morning my beautiful wife but there was no reply from her has I approached her bed to my horror I noticed that her left eye was open and sort of looking at me as though she was crying out for me to help her I stood there stunned I could not believe was I was seeing it could have been my Imagination making me see that her left eye was still open it looked so very real "so real" that I had this terrible and strange feeling in my mind that my dearest beautiful wife was asking me to help her it felt so very real its so hard to try and explain to any body unless they were there at that tragic moment in time, I slapped my face to pull myself together and held her hand which was cold I bent down and kissed her and placed my head on her left shoulder for a few moments suddenly the bed room felt so very cold and a dark cloud suddenly appeared out of no were above my dear wife, at first I thought it was this evil death wish curse aura stalking me again, noun aura meaning a general feeling of something evil surrounding this hospital bedroom were my dear wife was lying dead, This aura death dark cloud surrounding this hospital wards bedroom is the same feeling that I had experienced while holding my dear brave deceased mothers hand in this hospice bedroom when she passed away and died tragically in this hospice bedroom, It was at that precise moment when I suddenly realized that my dearest beautiful wife was dead I just could not get it into my head that my dearest beautiful wife who I was holding in my arms had tragicly died I just could not hold back my emotions much longer I was totally lossed and did not know what to do I could not stay with my dear wife any longer as my grief for the tragic loss of my beautiful wife was to much for me too handle and bear any longer I needed some fresh air and a cigarette I left my dearest wife and went out side for a cigarette and fresh air but it was very windy and raining very hard but I did not care about the weather or anything else in the world I felt like I was standing in an empty dark long tunnel with no light shinning at the end of it my life felt so empty and my heart was shattered into a million pieces the darkness over shadowed my entire body I was a lonely and a lossed soul, my entire life was shattered never in my entire life did I ever accept that my wife my dearest beautiful wife would pass away and tragically die before me I just could not get into my head that my beautiful wife was dead I had to go out side for some fresh air and a cigarette it pouring down with rain I did not care one bit and just stood there smoking my cigarette I was like a lossed soul just standing alone in the pouring rain trying to smoke a cigarette not knowing what to do, It was not until two women patients of this hospital who just finished smoking a cigarette and who had already heard that my wife had died went back up stairs to the ward and informed a staff nurse who was searching for me that I was standing out side in the pouring rain total upset and looking confused she immediately came out side and saw me standing in the pouring rain the staff nurse got hold of me and asked me if was ok I answered I don't really know she said that we have been trying to find you please come back in side the hospital with me as the sister in charge of the ward would like to have a word with you about your wife, I followed the staff nurse of this ward back into the hospital to see the sister in charge of this hospitals ward, the sister told me that a nurse who was looking after my wife went to wake up your wife as usual to have a bath once she knew that was awake the nurse told her to stay in bed while she gets her bath ready I could not believe what I was hearing I asked the sister in charge of this ward why was there only one nurse and not the usual two nurses looking after my wife while one nurse stays with my bed ridden wife who was on morphine to help with her cancer pain while the other nurse goes to the wards bathroom to make ready the bath to give my wife a usual morning bath, the ward sister replied that all of the wards other nursing staff are very busy making beds ready for the doctors morning rounds and that this nurse his a highly trained and a qualified and confident nurse my answer was then if thats so how come my wife is lying dead in her hospital bed and why in hells name did this highly trained and qualified confident nurse wake my wife up first before making ready this wards bathrooms bath for my wife's usual morning bath, I was very angry and that I believe that if there had been the two usual morning nurses attending and looking after my dear wife I believe that she would still have been alive this morning 12th August 2001, Its so tragic and difficult for me to believe that it was only yesterday when I visited my dearest wife as I usually do ever day and evening time to be with my dearest wife yesterday to take her out side for some fresh air and a cigarette she seamed ok and also when myself and my son visited his mother and my wife last night she once again seamed fine and ok she was even smiling and happy to see us both, It brings tears to my eyes and is breaking my heart that this morning 12th August 2001 that my dearest wife is no longer with me and our dear son I just cannot believe that my sons mother and my happy wonderful wife of thirty five years + happily married life together is now lying dead this morning 12th August 2001 in this hospital I just cannot get it into my head why my dear wife was left on her own while she was still on this medication morphine to help ease her cancer pain tried to get out of bed on her own but the side effects of the morphine would make my wife feel hallucination this is also known as visual hallucination feeling very confused dizziness and blurred vision disorientation definition people with cancer like my wife on morphine when woken up and roused from a deap sleep will be feeling very confused and disoriented and don't know where they are so my wife being confused and disoriented because of the morphine she was on to help ease the cancer pain would think that she was in bed at home got out of bed on her own with no nurse there to help her has she tried to get out of bed on her own she would have because of the morphine got dizzy and collapsed and as she fell of the bed she hit the sharp corner of the beds side cabinet very hard with her forehead noun the part of the face above the eyes the Staff Nurse who woke my wife up and left her alone while she made ready the bath heard my dearest wife scream and shouting for some one to help her when the Staff Nurse rushed into the bedroom she found my wife lying on the bedroom floor in a really bad state and bleeding badly from her forehead the nurse could see that my wife was unconscious adjective in the state of not being awake as the result of a head injury, from what I was told that within a few minutes the wards sister in charge of ward B and a staff nurse entered the room as they heard my wife screaming and crying for some body to help her but it was the Staff Nurse checked my wife's pulse there was no response so they immediately pressed the hospital emergency quick response teams red botton and within a matter of minutes they arrived and tried to bring my wife's heart back to life with a defibrillator that sends an electric shock to the heart but with no success, it was so very hard for me to realy at that specific moment in time to comprehend verb mentally understand that my dearest most beautiful wonderful wife my princess who's heart bloomed like a flower and touched every ones heart that she met had suddenly passed away and tragically died, the tragic death of my late dearest wonderful beautiful wife was a very difficult time in my life I was at a total loss for words I felt so emotional and close to tears my heart was broken into a million pieces it is and was the most painful tragic and saddest day of my whole life, a day I shall never ever forget as long as I shall live, I could not believe that my dearest beautiful wife was lying in a hospital bed on this ward dead it did not seam real that this could be happing to me that I have tragically lossed the life and heart of my life, my most wonderful beautiful wife so soon it was so sudden that my wife had passed away I just could not believe it as we were happily married for 35 magical wonderful years and have been together for 37 years in total, it was such a terrible shock to me, my son and my grandson I really had to try very hard to pull myself together as I had my son and grandson to think about but how does one hide this terrible grief, tragity, pain, sorrow and a broken heart from my son and grandson, I am a very proud man and served my country of the UK, in the armed military forces service's the R.A.F. but on this terrible sad occasion I will have to forgo being a proud man for the sake of my son and grandson as they shall need my full support, on this sad tragic occasion, I shall have to focus on dealing with the tragic loss and death of my beautiful dearest wonderful wife, It was 14 days later that my dearest beautiful wifes funeral took place on the 25th of august 2001 it was a very moving and most tragic moment in my life to see the funeral coffin that my dearest beautiful wife was lying dead I am a proud man but on this tragic day it was really difficult for me to hold back my tears and my entire bodies emotions, But her death shall not be in vain as I have written about her in this Fact-based true story in this book about the tragic death of my late wife and my brother and why I am still alive when I should have died many times over as I really have been on several occasions very close to the Brink of Death and close to the Gates of Hell, but that damnation evil eye is a specific type of mythical curse that someone wished this damnation evil eye terrible curse which his believed to cause, harm, illness, and even death upon us I was once a skeptical type of person adjective not easily convinced that something is true such has someone wishing and putting a curse on someone, but I now know and believe and understand now that most awful things are quite possible and that an evil death wished curse wished upon on a person can come true, because both my English mother and my eldest brother have both died a terrible tragic death, my mother tragically died of terminal cancer and my eldest brother died tragically of gangrene about myself well I have faced death in the face and I have been close to the Brink of Death and the Gates of Hell and walked away from both Death and Hell maybe its just luck or that I am destined to live on for a purpose such as a mission that from the proceeds of this book to become a humanitarian mission project charity welfare ambassador to help ease the suffering of the poor and underprivileged unfortunate homeless Orphan vulnerable children of this world, and to help the many Poorest of the poor people. The homeless people who are homeless through no fault of there own, And most importantly the many Hospices support care nurses who deal with a lot of terminally ill patients such as really young children and people suffering from terminal cancer Ext, this is a vital mission that I have dreamed of doing for such a very long time since the tragic loss and death of my late wife who died On the 12th August 2001 with terminal cancer, To continue but needed the assets to proceed with my humanitarian welfare charity project, with lots of luck with this Actual Events Fact-based True Story Book Titled From the Brink of Death and the Gates of Hell that I have been writing for over two years could be my salvation from its proceeds to start and full fill my dreams of this humanitarian charity welfare Charity Cause As Its Welfare Charity Ambassador, that is what I wish for as I know what its like to suffer and face death in the face and how people live in poverty and loneliness and struggle financially, I have experienced this at first hand the day I lossed my beautiful who died so tragically with terminal cancer who I was married too for over 35 years, It was then that I understood what loneliness and the struggle of every day life is, I did not want to live and tried to end my life by drinking lots and lots of beer, but it never worked out to my dismay,

[[THE YEAR WAS 2002 A YEAR THAT MY LIFE CHANGED FOR THE GOOD AS WRITTEN IN THE FOLLOWING STORY BELOW]]

As my story goes It was one day when my son said to me why don't you search on line for a dating agency I looked at him and said how can I do that I have no computer he said don't worry dad I I have a spare computer tower and a monitor up stairs which he bought down from his bedroom and set it up for me to use soon I was searching online for a foreign dating agency as I was searching this foreign dating agency I came across a photograph and a profile of this beautiful looking foreign woman and her email address telephone number and her home address were she lived in this pictuesque scenic charming beautiful city of Naberezhnye located somewhere in the north-eastern part of Tatarstan, there was something about this photo and her profile that I like very much I immediately decided to write to her and tell her about myself and also send her my photograph, telephone number e mail address, and my home address here in the UK, when I had finished writing my letter to this beautiful foreign looking woman I immediately took it to the main post office located somewhere in this busy north seaside coastal resorts town of north-west Lancashire the UK, having done that I waited for a reply from this beautiful foreign woman once she received my letter to reply to me via my email address or a letter from her by postal service, well after a couple of days I received an email from this beautiful looking foreign woman I was over the moon it was so good to read her email but also I could not believe the tragic emotional story she wrote in her email about her tragic emotional cruel life she had suffered at the hands of her drunken alcoholic foreign husband and how he tried very hard to kill her by trying to strangle her to death and would have succeeded if it had not been for her son who had come home early from work he heard is mothers cry for help and rushed into the apartment flat just in time and pulled his drunken alcoholic father of his mother he then immediately telephoned for an ambulance as is mother was in a state of shock, the full near death tragic story that she has written below explains how she and her two beautiful children, her beautiful young daughter and her handsome young son have suffered so much with there drunken alcoholic father's drunken bad habits and in is drunken state shouts abusive words and gets very angry and starts arguing with their mother, Her life before she met meaning meet her foreign husband had a very happy life as a young girl living in this foreign vast enormous and extremely large city located somewhere in Eastern Europe with her mother her father and her two elder sisters and two brothers, but her happy life was to change and end when she moved from this vast enormous and extremely large city were herself and her two sisters and brothers were born and bred located in this vast enormous and extremely large foreign country of Eastern Europe and relocated to this vast enormous and extremely large new city of Naberezhnye located somewhere in the north-eastern part of Tatarstan were she met noun meet her future foreign husband she married him at a young age of 23 in this city of this vast enormous and extremely large country of Naberezhnye located somewhere in the north-eastern part of Tatarstan, I have already mentioned above that her ex husband was a drunken alcoholic and her married life to him was fraught with difficulties and abuse due to his drunken state and alcohol abuse he even tried to strangle her to death who has two beautiful young children from her marriage to her husband a beautiful daughter and a handsome son their mother worded all the time in this electronics factory to be able to support her two young children her daughter and son, her daughter became a teacher and her son became an engineer, they are both married and live in the family home where they were both raised in this city of this vast enormous and extremely large foreign country of Naberezhnye located somewhere in the north-eastern part of Tatarstan, but unfortunately their financial circumstances is very bad as work is very difficult and hard to find and if lucky enough to find work the wage is only about on average 100 dollars a month which in English money is only about 60 pounds to pay the rent to look after their family and to buy food ext,

[[TO FINALIZE AND END THE WRITTEN CHAPTERS IN THIS BOOK TITLE FROM THE BRINK OF DEATH AND THE GATES OF HELL, THE FINAL CHAPTER IN THIS BOOK IS ABOUT MY RUSSIAN WIFE'S TRAGIC STORY THAT I HAVE ALLOWED HER TO WRITE, HER OWN STORY IN THIS BOOK AS FOLLOWS BELOW,]]

To continue from above my dear beautiful russian wife is writing her own genuine real-life actual Fact-based events true story in this book titled from the brink of death and the gates of hell, from her memoirs meaning memory about her sad and unhappy married life, but also her happy life which is a Fact-based events true story that my wife has written from her private memoirs about herself her two sisters and brothers happy young life while living in this vast enormous and extremely large foreign city were we were born and bred located somewhere in Eastern Europe, To continue this is my wife's Fact-based True Events Story as follows, I was born in this vast enormous and extremely large foreign city located somewhere east-central Europe, there were five children in our family my two elder sisters and two younger brothers and myself my father was a beekeeper my mother bless her looked after all of us we lived in a forest near a village called circle the village is in the shape of a circle and surrounded by hills there was a beautiful forest lots of flowers animals and also very clean spring water my family roots are from this vast enormously large country of Poland a country in East-Central Europe because my grandfather was a foreign immigrant he was married with a foreign women they had a big farm including an apiary which was home to a lot of peasants they were the prosperous peasants we helped our father in the apiary unfortunately in 1933 this evil leader picked out everything they had and banishment to was not a civilized place of east-centrat that time so my family began to live some where in east central Europe, Over the years my father worked at a big company as an accountant, but leaved this job and became as a beekeeper as did his father he loved his business very much and called the bees his children we had a small farm with many types of domestic animals there were chickens geese ducks turkeys rabbits sheep including two dogs and two cats My two sisters and me helped our parents to work in the garden because we had a big land and growing a lot of vegetables The summer in east-central Europe is very warm and pleasant every day I have seen beautiful exciting nature my mum taught us to take care of nature and its beauty, in winter nature is really very beautiful there is lots of snow – and we would roll in the snow we made and played with snow balls and also we used to ski a lot every time when I think about my childhood my memoirs noun memory bring me to a magical fairy tail I remember every corner every path in the forest where I grew beautiful white berches trees with their wonderful scent blowing in the warm breeze especially in the evening after a hot summer's day there was a stream near the forest we had to cross the steam by a small bridge to get to our house which was deap in the forest in the forest was a source of spring water the spring water had a peculiar taste and was very cold' like just from the fridge, around the stream there were a lot of bird cherries and in the spring when the flowers were flowering there was such a beautiful view of the trees as though the snow on the branches got mixed up with the green leaves and the air was fragrant with a smell of flowers My father my two sisters and myself wake up at four o clock in a morning and mow the grass people used to say make hay while the sun shines that is why at ten o clock in the morning's the grass become dried up and it was so very hard to cut it when the hay was dried up and was ready we collected it and put it into a hay loft my father took a horse from a village to help my mother said don't be lazy to help us otherwise we have nothing to eat in winter she teaches us never be afraid and always to have you opinions in fact we were often short of money I remember when our father bought apples and oranges for us only once a year to celebrate new year I remember the smell of the fruits like the smell of my childhood, the people always have a strong spirit and hardships but are very hospitable and always with open heart and soul when my father bought the ski for us I was very afraid to stand on the ski but I was very quick to learn how to use the ski so that I can be able to slide and ski down the snow covered hill which took my breath away and only the wind was whistling behind me and I wanted to ski more an more down the snow covered mounting, so from season to season we were both very happy and enjoyed communication with nature and with each other this was my happy childhood and my earthly paradise We had to go from our village as I was at age of 16 we moved to a big city in east-central Europe, It was only five miles away from our village that we moved from too this big city some where in east-central Europe, we should hopefully be able to get an education my dream was to become a veterinary surgeon or a scientist to learn deaply about nature and its wild life such as the many birds and natures wild life animals but unfortunately this university was so far from our city and my parents could not pay rent for some place for me to live in to continue my two oldest sisters studied in college at that time and my two young brothers continued at school So I was looking for a job to help my parents support the family financially I eventually found a job at the train passenger's depot I had a crash course as a passenger guide I was then 17 years old and I had travelled very much on the passenger trains all around I really loved it and I found that it was very romantic and interesting for me I loved when in my life happened many good events I like a challenge and I want to get over, my journey was continued on the train which had stopped at the train station and the many east-central Europe picturesque beautiful Scenic Cities of east-cantral Europe, I used to love to look out of the window of the warm train carriage and saw the beauty of my country some times the frost was 40c on the out side of the warm train carriages there was always two train guides to a carriage as we both had to keep the train carriage warm there was a fire place in the carriage and we used coal to keep the fire burning continuously, There was 14 carriages being pulled by the electric or diesel train we had a big team about sixty people including a team leader and an electrician on the train in case of electrical problems we looked after many people re Train passengers making sure that we put coal in the fire in the fire place on the train to help keep all of the passengers warm after cleaning the passenger train carriage we made a cup of tea for the passengers in the morning and also in the evening even though there was a dinning car on the train were they could buy something to eat and drink it was very nice to work in summer on the train as a conductor especially travelling to some where in the south of east-central Europe on the train were a lot of holiday makers who got off the train to visit and see the black-sea of east-central Europe, When our train and cleaners got it ready to travel in the opposite direction to its arrived at its destination of east-central Europe, a special team of engineers next destination in east-central Europe, while all this was happening my colleagues and I got a few hours off to go to the a city or go to the beach in the south of east-central Europe, there is a very stylish nature named the Caucasus mounting there peaks were covered with snow white clouds lie on the slopes of the mountings I reach out with my arms and want to touch the white clouds with my hands, the valleys near the Caucasus mountings are covered with a lot of beautiful flowers and on the beach the golden sands and the black sea is a very bright blue colour I love the Caucasus mountings they are beautiful and very mighty and mysterious they are like a magnet that pull up and conquerorn of the people, as a person said better the mountings can be only mountings on which you have never been, after two years of my work on the railway a director offered me the position as a team leader on the train my parents were against my idea they said that it is a very big responsibility and that I was only

20 years old and could not to run a risk I really understand and knew that I would be responsible for the train and passengers on the train and for the team So I told my parents don't worry about it and that everything will be alright I loved my work on the train as a conductor and that it was really exciting me to be a train and passenger team leader during my work as a train and passenger team leader I had many different cases happened, such as once as I was travelling to east-central Europe and to this east-central Europe city, it was deap midnight before going to bed I had to check the passenger carriagies to be sure that everything is alright on the train when I passed through some carriages and looked at next carriage it was on fire I knew that if I don't liquidate the fire quickly the carriage can burn with passengers trapped for fifteen minutes I had a terrible shock and fear I stopped the train and I had to out of the carriage and saw burning a storage battery under neath the carriage I told my colleagues don't panic and make a noise some passengers helped us to liquedante the fire we were terrified the train stopped in this east-central taiga forest which was so very far from locality, it was dark and a calm night there was only night lights in the carriages shinning out of the carriages windows into the dark night for this case me and my two colleagues were paid compensation, my director said he was very thankful for us and the very first important thing was that we saved peoples life and that we also saved the train carriage during my work at the railway I sorted many cases on the railway carriages I am happy that I made the right decision I know that everybody burns with there own personal strife but their addition to go on in a family and in surroundings and I knew what I have in my character purposeful will power optimism kindness love all that gave me and my sisters and my brothers and our mum and dad first of all we had work and education as in every villages some where in east-central Europe were four five six or more family at that time we had a big land and a lot of domestic animals to feed a big family, from a little age about

seven years old we helped our parents to work the land we had not got any farming machines to help farm the big land also we helped to look after all of the animals and in the summer we made a stock for winter and hay for two cows and a few sheep anyway I go to work on the railway as a conductor and one day I met my future husband on the train he was serving in this foreign army for two years, and when he came back we decided to get married one year later we have a baby and I left my job on the railway, and we moved to the center of this picturesque scenic charming city of this vast enormous and extremely large country of Naberezhnye located somewhere in the north-eastern part of Tatarstan, Myself and my husband both had a job at a big factory were I worked at in the electronic repair department and my husband worked as a builder we had a two bedroom flat and three years on we have a son it seamed everything we alright but not my husband had got the friends in his team and often came home late from work drunk" though I asked him many times to come back home to a normal life he promised me that he would but he never did keep his promise and ever time he become aggressive and try to beat me I called the cities local police but they say that they could not arrest him has they had no evidence regarding him beating me he made my life hell I could not too leave him as I had not enough money to rent another flat my children and I lived in fear often he would try to attack me with a knife myself and my children stayed in our neighbours flat and waited for when he went to bed" when we went into our flat it would stink of cigarettes and vodka it came to the point that our relationship was finally broken and at an end during the ten years before the divorce we lived in separate rooms when my children were grown up my daughter studied in the university and my son in the college, finally I then made for a divorce and after the divorce things got much worse with my drunken husband one day when my two children were out he tried to strangle me and I could not breath I tried to call some body help me suddenly my son came home and pulled him away from me and called to an ambulance as I was in a big shock I put in an application to police and judge told me that my ex husband he will send to prison for three years, then my ex husband was standing on his knees and asking me to for give him and promise never ever to touch me again what ever happens, I forgive him because I am a good natured person fortunately he had some work in a little town near our city, and came home only for a few days.

Finally to summarize the end of my Real-life Fact-based true events story From the Brink of Death and the Gates of Hell that I have written in this book about the many tragic evil events and challenges that both myself and my beautiful foreign wife have struggled with through out both of our sad and sometimes tragic life, How do you stop the grieving tears filling your eyes how do I get over the wonderful magical moments I shared for over thirty five magical glories years with my late deceased beautiful wife, and the magical times I had with my late deceased eldest brother how do I express my emotions feelings and tears for my late deceased brave courages English mother who fought so bravely to keep us all alive, its really difficult to come to terms with the tragic loss of both my beautiful wife who passed away and tragically died on August 12th 2001 with terminal cancer and my eldest brother who passed away and died tragically five months later on the 30th January 2002 not long after the funeral of my late deceased beautiful wife on the 25th August every moment of my life I think and look at and read my book that I have written Titled From The Brink of Death And The Gates of Hell grievies me so much and tears fill my eyes and when I look at my late wife and my late brothers photograph's, and my late English mother and step fathers photographs tears fill my sad grieving eyes and my bodies every emotions fills me with grief and lots of sadness as it does every Christmas and every anniversaries that passes by every new year. Finally the saying goes that to many tears fills your heart with sadness but in my case my tears not only fill my heart with sadness but also happiness of the many irreplaceable good times I shared with my late deceased wife,

THE END